D1192848

The Book
ON...

and Jesus answers

The Book ON...
and Jesus Answers

By Joel Wright

978-0-9767485-1-9

Published by Project Healing Press

All rights reserved. No parts of this book may be reproduced or
transmitted in any form or by any means, electronic or mechanical,
including photocopying, recording or by any information storage and
retrieval system, without written permission from the author,
except for the inclusion of brief quotations in a review.

Printed in the United States of America

Copyright © 2008 WLH LLC
Published 2009

Edited By: Premakarini

Cover and Interior Design:
Susan Sylvia, Staircase Press Design

ISBN 978-0-9767485-1-9

Project Healing Press
St. Louis, Missouri
www.projecthealingpress.com

The Book
ON
and Jesus answers

as scribed by Joel Wright

ON

Global Warming

and

Practicing the Cycle of Healing

and

A Message from Joel

scribed by Mary Gerard

In her desire and willingness to be truly helpful,
Mary pauses, turns toward God within and receives
The words of Jesus and Holy Spirit.

Opening her heart and mind to the Love God Is
And sharing this Love as Guided,
in thought, word, and deed.

Together we are being healed in ways seen and unseen,
as we realize, Love is all there Is

TABLE OF
CONTENTS

ON...

ON...

Editor's note

It is a privilege and a blessing to have worked so closely
with this material with Jesus. Having experienced its
healing and transformational power from reading and
rereading this book as part of the editorial process, I feel
moved to encourage you to read and reread this book often,
so you can fully absorb the power of the love that comes
through Jesus' words, allowing these words to gently guide
you into reality and out of illusion.

We are so blessed to have such a book that allows Jesus to
communicate so directly bringing his timeless wisdom into
our world today with such clarity, love and grace.

I have been so blessed to have Jesus in my life since I was
a child, so it did not surprise me when I was asked to edit
and help with this book. Right away I knew that Jesus spoke
clearly through Joel, the love is palpable; I am so happy to
share this with you. I only edited where necessary,
and only with Jesus.

With love and blessings,
Premakarini
Author of Jesus' Love

ACKNOWLEDGMENTS

Thank you to Jesus, for your love and blessings,
and for being with us always.

Many thanks to Premakarini for her editorial
contribution and assistance in getting this material
out in the world.

Thank you to Mary Gerard for listening
with the Holy Spirit and scribing the Foreword
and for bringing Jesus' message on *Global Warming* and
Practicing the Cycle of Healing which are excerpts
from her upcoming book,
Visions of Illumination, Seeing With the Mentor Within.
And for receiving *A Message from Joel*
after Joel's transition.

Many thanks to Sue Sylvia for your kind support
and service producing this book and cover design.

Thank you to Carol Hamilton for her gracious
and valuable legal assistance

John Hutkin is grateful to be given the opportunity,
with Joel's blessing,
to help bring this book into this world.
And receiving the grace to be willing to be truly helpful
and receive the vision of the cover design
along with Sue Sylvia.
Participation in the editorial assistance and the supporting
of the production of *The Book ON* is a blessing.

Thank you, Joel, for your willingness
to allow me to serve God by serving you.

Here is an acknowledgement from Joel,
received after his transition, through John.

*I stand in gratitude to my sister, Sherry Wright,
and my daughter, Paula Wright,
for their presence in my life.*

Joel

FOREWORD

You hold within your hands the power to change everything that is happening in the world simply by choosing to awaken from the dream of illusion. It is only you who gives power to the dream illusion you think is your world. The Book On is here to share the way out of illusion with you, the way to live in Love instead of the illusions of fear and suffering in your world now.

A reality of love, peace and truth is already here and is waiting for you to experience it now. You need only be willing.

Be willing to listen and turn within to experience your true Divine Self.

This is what the Book On shares with you: Joel listens with his heart and receives Jesus' timeless wisdom so we can know how it serves the world today.

Jesus unceasingly serves us all, ever bringing us into truth; this is his love and devotion to us. He is with us eternally. This is his service and devotion to each and every one of us. Jesus loves us with love that is infinite, and when we receive this love, we share it with the world.

All we need to do is be willing to humbly receive this truth.

Joel has brought the light of truth before us in *The Book On*; as we receive it, it is shared with the world.

Blessings in the light of love,
Premakarini with Jesus

Love speaks directly in these pages of the unwinding of time as the past fades away, the future disappearing before we even seem to arrive and we are moved into the reality of now—All That Is. Come with certainty and reap the sharing of Jesus and the extending of his love, given to one who said "Yes," to the wisdom of willingness. Willingness to take pause from his own way and *listen* to the way of Love.

Questions arise in our minds about the nature of the world and the choices we seem to face. Violence, attack, freedom misunderstood, knowledge unknown, power misinterpreted, bodies sick of themselves, minds at war, ego fraught with its mistaken identity, the purpose of relationships remaining unfulfilled and judgment laid down upon others and ourselves as if forgiveness was a forgotten language. One problem appearing as many—one decision made to make a world of our own, on our own. There is one solution.

Love is always with us; we only have to listen. So advanced is our listening potential, were each of us to cultivate it, the world would quiet the moment we all *listened*. The listening of which I speak is the listening demonstrated here in Joel's scribing. *Listening to the Presence of God—in our oneness with this Love.* Joy is the experience of following Love, for in our following, love is shared. These pages leap with true joy because they are sharing love. In extending Love, the appearances of the world and all of our suffering over them are gone. Light replaces the darkness. The reality of Love has our complete awareness.

Our freedom of choice is our ticket into darkness or our flight into the Light. We decide. Jesus is love—a demonstration of love not of the world that comes into the world through an open heart and willing mind—one leading into the other for they are one in the same in Spirit. The mind asleep in unwillingness, separation and despair has no ground to stand on in our willingness to trust Love. We will be glad when we take our flight into the Light and the fruits of our freedom are ripe with love. In sharing this love we will be an inspiration to all hearts desiring to open who know not yet that their *Self is at one with Love.* Joel is demonstrating that everyone can hear the Voice for God. Ask and we shall receive.

Truly,
Mary Gerard *listening* to *The Mentor Within*

DEAR JESUS...
FROM JOEL

Dear Jesus,

What steps are needed on my part
for the successful publication and distribution
of the material you are offering through me?

Dearest Joel,

You are scribing this material as I have instructed, and have listened well and completed this part of the assignment. What you are receiving is for everyone, including you. And, indeed, it is for you first, because you, along with my Help, will be representing God, the Great Cause of all life and meaning.

Communication is key to the success of any true cause. In communicating, you must allow the Holy Spirit as our Voice, to flow seamlessly through, without your being sidetracked into secondary concerns, such as the problems you sometimes encounter in relationship to the world of illusions. To you, and to everyone, the world seems very real, while communication from Heaven seems as if to be whimsical and fluffy information; that is, information you may judge on your own to be sometimes worthy and sometimes not, depending on where your emphasis is being placed at the time.

You all tend to lose focus, and THAT is the main problem of the world. The ego takes what it wants and most often judges what it thinks you don't immediately need. I say to you now, you NEED every piece of information I am sending through you. You NEED to have full willingness to share this information in the most sincere way possible. Its taken importance will make or break the future as you see it.

I have said there is no future, but only the present instant. Yet most, including you, are busy planning your next day, the ego's "survival," and all that the ego tells you is worthy of protecting and upholding. NONE OF ITS JUDGMENT IS GENUINE OR REAL, and is merely the ego's method for sidetracking your function and your true purpose.

The money, the things, and all that you physically see and behold, are merely a part of a seemingly shared dream. As you take this dream more seriously, the dream turns into a nightmare, and worse yet, hell on earth! You do not want the dream, its past and future perceptions and judgment!

It IS perception (all perception, good or bad) that you need escape FROM. Perception makes time, and time is without meaning and cause, for it has no substance, and stands only on a broken foundation. The value of such a foundation determines the sense of separation you feel from God, me, and all brothers and sisters. It is perception that needs undoing. ALL perception! Without its undoing, your life would be a living hell. You must teach others and thus learn for yourself, that refuge from the dream of the world is ALL that is important for you.

All suffering stems from living this dream, for it is none but a lack of love. Start by realizing NOW that there is no past or future. Your escape begins in this recognition. And you will all escape together, simply by sharing the recognition that Heaven is nowhere without YOU.

You must discipline your mind to release constantly from all perception and the seeming need to think behind or ahead. The guilt and pain you all feel is because you are unwilling to follow this simple instruction. I came once and performed miracles by holding this recognition in my own heart and mind. As I shared it I strengthened it in all others. You must learn to follow in my footsteps, for YOU are the world's only hope.

Therefore, waste no more time on trivia, survival issues and inventive thinking. This thinking takes you away from your joy and your shared happiness. GIVING without condition is your one escape from this tunnel of darkness and despair.

Do not judge for yourself who or when to give the Father's Love. I will decide for you and for all. You need light, and you can find and experience it IF you will follow these instructions. Your thinking must be left behind in as far as what and how you think alone and on your own. Ours is a shared purpose, and every other purpose is wasted.

DO NOT WANT. All will be taken care of if you look within to the Father of all compassion and unity for answers!

There is but one mission for all of you while on earth: to learn of your unity with God and Christ, and to give only this. If someone asks you for something else, give it to them if you have it to give, for they believe they need it, and you know that you don't.

Freedom lies not in arguing or disagreeing, but in each person's willingness to help and love beyond what you "value" in the world and in things!

Understand, THE WORLD IS UNDONE ALREADY, BUT YOU WILL NOT EXPERIENCE IT OR KNOW IT FOR YOURSELF UNLESS YOU SHARE THE SPIRIT FROM WHICH YOU CAME.

For our material to be successful, you need to place emphasis on what I have just told you. Otherwise, hypocrisy can only enter, and more darkness can only follow. It may be hard at first to give of what you often most value. Yet, if you do not participate in the practice as I have just described, how will the world remember Heaven?

Your part is essential for salvation. Without you, no one could remember God's abundant truth! Without exception child of Light, THIS you need to practice in all you think and all you do. What you think determines the actions you take.

Give the Holy Spirit your thinking, and He will bring through your thinking as it is undone only the light of truth, the sharing of His Abundance and the happy dance you all share together on the one road Home! And by the way, your success IS indeed my promise to you all!

In Peace,

Jesus

PREFACE

Though the following question and answer may be viewed as profound, and at first difficult to understand, it is recommended that you read it once now and then come back to it again later as you proceed further into this material.

What did you mean when you said, "my God, my God, why hast Thou forsaken me?"

Imagine the intensity of my being crucified. It looks quite devastating as viewed by the ego. But I was not looking at it from such a timely vantage point. I saw only a call for love, and in return I offered them my deepest blessing: "Father forgive them, they know not what they do." I could not see my Self as being wounded as a result. My interest was only in demonstrating to those who believed they were hurting me, and thus themselves by the apparent projection of attack by their egos, that attack is impossible.

That is why this blessing is both protective and profound when understood correctly. The supposed crimes of the ego, and the apparent intensity of the attack are no different. Both mean nothing at all, because they are doing nothing at all. Yet it is obvious in time that this was not what was being believed and thus seen.

It should be understood just by the testimony of the apostles that the ego (worldly mind) is incapable of understanding anything. The glorification of my body and the emphasis on its suffering is seen everywhere, even to this day. And this will go on until the belief in separation is undone on a large scale. Then, looking back, it will be fully understood that suffering of any kind is truly impossible.

Though the fact that the ego cannot understand anything is true, the ego can comprehend suffering because the ego is an example of the belief in suffering. The statement, "My God, my God, why hast Thou forsaken me?" is thus the final proof. It seems incomprehensible to the ego that the Son of God could have made such a statement. And that is because the statement was made at such an ultimate level, that the ego must find it impossible to both lovingly decipher and understand.

Yet, if you will look ever so quietly at this statement, you may recognize its eternal ultimateness, as well as the deeply loving final message of human frailty that can never be reconciled unto Christ in Heaven.

The statement was a final exclamation of the absolute impossibility of reconciliation between the ego and God. Understood in this way, it brings to you one of the most powerful messages I came to bring. That is, the message of offering only complete blessing and mercy to every human being you would meet.

The final Gift I could give in the illusory realm of human existence was a firm declaration which bore witness to the final reign of the ego's seeming ability to inflict suffering. The lesson: punishment is reasonless and blessing is everything.

You may better understand this lesson now by quietly stepping back and calmly asking yourself, "Who is the 'me' called 'I'?" The part of you whom you call 'I' is the only part that seems capable of any suffering. Yet it is not you.

You are in Christ with me, and so we are One eternally. If you will contemplate this ultimate fact carefully, then you will easily understand the statement, "My God, my God, why hast Thou forsaken me?" God could never forsake what you truly are, because as part of Christ you are everything.

God did forsake your ego the moment it was thought possible to experience it. Understood in this way, the final statement assures you of your own perfect and eternal blessing, for what you are with me and all brothers can never be forsaken.

One further point must be made regarding this greatly misunderstood question. When the statement was made, "My God, my God, why hast Thou forsaken me?" the blessed and complete comfort of God's final Answer was instantly given and received forever; "Because you are Christ, my Son, with Whom I am well pleased."

As this final Answer was given and received, the circle of our own Atonement was completed. Christ the King was anointed, and His rightful Crown, the Crown of everlasting Light are bestowed unto the sons and daughters for all to share. By this, no longer do you need fear being forsaken by God, ever.

Through the resurrection that followed, and past the Day of days, for now and forever, we live in Christ together in a Circle that is complete. Would you not then receive the same Gift to share with me now? For with me, we are all One, forever in Christ together.

Bliss and Light...

Jesus

The Book
ON

and Jesus answers

INTRODUCTION

We continue in Truth to answer many questions that are commonly shared in regard to religion, spirituality, the purpose of relationships, and the mortality and yet immortality they inevitably must unveil.

And in between each of your questions, there is a story being told: a story about your own unassailable and wholly lovable creation. Unlike the world, this story, though mythical it may sound, is not a myth at all. It is about you.

A Course In Miracles is a book that is solely designed for undoing the mind's fear, and returning it to the awareness of Love from which it came. *The Mirror On Still Water* followed, and offers practical guidance to those seeking to apply spiritual principles and listen to the Holy Spirit within the seeming complication of the world's setting.

The Book ON still furthers this practical assistance, but with a more direct and specific wisdom for bringing about true peace in the world, not for a few but for the many.

Many miracle workers are gathering, some as a result of *A Course In Miracles* study, and many from other studies, teachings and ways. There is a reason for this, as there is for everything each of you are now experiencing. The coming of great illumination is upon you. There is also great struggle amongst you in bringing this about. It is being given to you that the struggle for freedom will complete itself. And complete itself it will.

The Book ON will offer all of you a corrective insight for practical living. It has been designed and inspired by He who gives Life to all. It is for you from Him through me. For only within you is the Power of Christ revealed. Yet see Him in your brother and sister first. For only through your reception of Him in all can you remember and understand the Great Magnitude of grandeur you share as one together. I join you there, now in *The Book ON*, and blessed are you who walk not alone.

Christ Jesus

ON
CREATION
AND
THE WORLD

Greetings from Christ and all the angels, and who are on high with you in our Father's Heaven.

Let us begin with a new explanation of creation and the world. The confusion between creation and the world is an example of how the Bible has been misinterpreted over time. God did not create the world, the days, months, years or anything you associate with time.

The eternal does not express itself in time, though when expressed, time will temporarily cease. Indeed, you know this because you are indeed eternal! You perhaps do not believe this because the picture show you are watching is darkened and yet bejeweled by the paintings of grandiosity, illusion, sorrow and death. Each eye beholds the sight of separation differently.

The world is not of Heaven. It is therefore not really alive in any sense. Nor has it any meaning above what you assign it. Every definition given to the material world was made up historically through time. Following were its rules and laws, all of which were, and are, all made up by you.

God did not create what you think and see. You made it all, and then defined it as a way to cope and communicate while in a state of mind that is indeed loveless and separate from God. This form of worldly communication is unreal to God, and therefore does not really exist.

The result is you falling asleep and dreaming a dream that you have come to accept as "reality." This dream has become so real to you that you are often devastated by every unexpected change. I have come to bring a gentle and forgiving perception to the hardness, despair and hatred.

Though the world is but a dark dream at best, you are capable of overlooking and thus transcending the darkness that appears all around you. You have been trained to do just the opposite and to take the world most seriously. I am come to teach you to laugh again, and thus, to heal the darkness and shine it away. Nothing of the world's perception is worthy of becoming upset over. Nothing.

Try to understand that the world you see is built on past history, definition and perception. You have built the world and its history by assigning word meanings to everything you see and experience. These definitions you have given to everything physical is a method for guaranteeing the survival of the body.

The world is therefore made by your definitions and made perceptions on behalf of those definitions. God did not create any of this. He did not make the physical. You and only you did. In this sense, the world's education is one of illusion and not reality.

The laws perception must follow appear stable, but as you know, often still fool you. This is because perception is pliable and bendable. It is therefore undependable because it is not consistent.

Certain scientific rules are more consistent, but only because they are based in natural and calculated reaction. However, even these can be adjusted and manipulated because their formulas are also perception based. The bottom line is that what you have made can never be perfectly consistent because what you have made can never rest in the eternal.

Try to understand it with this simplicity. God created you as eternal beings. Life is not determined by the body, for this is merely the ego's home. The ego sees itself as separate from everyone and God, trying its best to survive all alone. This, again, is perception based.

To counter this perception, miracles are needed to be introduced within the separation to remind you on occasions that perception, separation and the physical are all merely part of complex ever-changing dream based in guilt and fear, getting and taking, using and abusing, and basically, acting in some form of lovelessness.

This is all merely part of a bad dream for you. You need to awaken but you don't know how. I am come to reawaken you to what you truly have and what you have truly always been. I am Jesus, and I've come to help you back to your real Home.

You are His creation. And because this cannot be changed, it is merely up to you when you are ready to let go completely and fully remember what you indeed are. Your lamp is lit. And I am standing in the light with you. Together we will simply remember to open our eyes and see the light that has always been our own together.

I am with you now. Trust in only my presence and abandon your attachment to the things and places you look out to. For they have already abandoned you and have never cared for you. You cannot count on one of them. You can, however, count on God in Heaven. He is your eternal Source. He has never left you, even while you sought comfort elsewhere. He has no hatred, but only love for all His creation.

Learn to listen to the gentle whisper of His Holy Spirit, come to return your confused mind to the sureness of Heaven's eternal Heart. This is your dwelling. This is your calling. Your Home gently awaits your glad return.

ON
EVOLUTION

What is evolution but a term for growth and change?

And is not growth and change a term that belongs only to the ego? For the ego is constantly inventing "new" ways in which the illusion of growth and change are permitted. And though growth and change are quite apparent on a physical level, the level of spirit is change-less indeed.

You are indeed growing back into the spirit of your own creation, since you are each overcoming your own tendencies to forget the truth about yourselves. Yet the truth of you does not change. You are a spirit residing temporarily in a body. Since of itself the body is not your reality, you could say that you are each experienc-ing this illusion for a time.

However, those of you who are truly interested in your own spiritual path must come to question the idea of evolution, since God has created each of you beyond the changes the ego always alludes to.

And it is this questioning that will surely lead each of you to God in the end. What you must learn to ques-tion is the very idea that any change in what you are is even possible.

When you have come to a place in your lives where each of you stops seeking change, and instead seeks only spirit, then the illusory changes of life will not affect you in the ways they once did. For change is of the world, but not of God who remains your constant Source. In this sense, you may begin to understand change as only a remembrance of what you truly are.

Each of you on earth are fully evolved. There is nothing for you to do except accept what you have and are in God. But do not see this a simple undertaking, for in the process you are asked to lose all those layers of fear and guilt that make up your seemingly separate identities.

And in this process you will be able to rejoin with one another while in the physical world. This rejoining is nothing short of a miracle. For, in fact, it is a miracle.

So in a sense, your rejoining with one another is your evolvement, which you all will get to experience together.

You may wonder how it is possible that all of humanity will ever see each other as joined? And herein lies the responsibility of the miracle worker. For in joining with one other person fully, many others will join with you, for joining is joyous, and joy is infectious.

ON
LANGUAGE

Each of you may have noticed that language is often not a barrier where affairs of the heart are concerned.

Could it be any different then in your communication with God? Setting down your dependency on your own made languages is a prerequisite for communicating with each other and your Creator.

Language, thus, that is made by you, is twice removed from the original language of communication created for you by your Creator. Love is not communicated through words, but instead through giving. Giving is also a way of receiving, and receiving a way to give.

Communication is silent, as it is ongoing in the spiritual sense. When you truly give to another you receive for both first. That is why learning to listen is everything, while speaking is notable only when giving is contained within its action. Silence is golden because within its premise is the light of truth and love.

Though a certain language always contains many self-made barriers to real communication, these can be easily overcome when both people are willing to look at their communication as one of two concepts: an offering of love or a call for love. There are many who are asking for many things they believe they are lacking in. And yet each is only calling for the reminder of their own Divinity.

It is a fact that the very world you seem to see is, in actuality, a calling for love. The world has no love, and is incapable of offering it. Look not to the world to answer your own calling, for it will fail you. Look instead within you, where a calm, steady and peaceful light shines. In constancy it is always there amidst all your battles, fights and disagreements. For language is but a barrier to the light that is a constant in you and your brothers and sisters.

The language you have made is but some form of wanting. But the language of God is always some form of sharing. This is why you should be a guard of what you speak, and for that matter, even what you may think.

But in silence, be willing to share your heart with everyone, for your heart will always speak for the mind if you will ask for spirit's inner guidance first. When the mind speaks it always speaks first because it is fearful. The heart may speak last, and it may speak of an alternative you find difficult to accept.

But remember this: The Holy Spirit knows no sacrifice is possible. You need only remember this in times you are tempted to think otherwise. And then, decide for Love with Love.

Remember that the language of the ego is fearful, for its concern is always with getting. But the language of the Holy Spirit is always loving because His concern is only with sharing, extending and giving. If you allow your will to be guided by only this, you will have no trouble remembering your own true nature. And you will know your Self and God's Will with each decision.

How does one listen to the Voice of God? By listening to your own heart. Your heart knows everything, and "speaks" in a different way than the mind. Your heart speaks of both knowledge and joy. It gently tells you that you are eternal and that you need not fear. The heart gently informs you that you need not change, and that you cannot change what you are. Merely in your acceptance of the true nature of your own creation can you silence the ego and its rants and ravings.

Usual language is not a necessity where the heart is concerned. The heart of your Self is where God abides, and He is gentle and without conditions. You may wonder why it seems so difficult at times to hear your Self and God. This is merely because most of you have layer upon layer of fear thoughts that your ego has made to protect the body.

And God's language is different. Rather than speaking with words, His language often comes in waves of joy and acceptance. It is a feeling, really. One which is full of unspeakable happiness and peace.

You may think you couldn't possibly have this kind of unlimited joy within your grasp. But that is the problem, you are thinking about how to find it, and thus, you are looking outside yourself for an Answer that can only be rediscovered from within.

So you see, dear one, that in order to truly hear your Self, your thinking must temporarily cease. And outer searching must also cease. You cannot see the light in another before you lay down the conditions and expectations you have placed on her. This is also true of your self.

As I have said, God does not necessarily hear you through merely the spoken word, although words can bring you closer or place you further from His inner communication. No matter what, when you are not in complete communication with Him He does hear your words as a call for love. And He answers you even though you may not be willing to hear Him. He answers with an offering of complete unconditional love and gentle reminders that you are indeed sinless and whole.

It is through your brother and sister that you will begin to understand the language of God. Without them you would be hopelessly lost in the ego's mire of darkness and fear. Through your acceptance of each of them as teachers, you will learn of Him Who has always loved and kept you.

For Heaven is always entered together or forgotten together. Listen to your sisters and brothers not with your own conditions but with an open heart. Each of them calls to you to enter Heaven with them, even while they may be angry or in discomfort. Each calls to you to help them in Love's remembrance. Would you not join with them in fulfilling God's most Holy Plan?

ON
MONEY

Cash, stocks, bonds, gold, silver, oil, land, houses, power and more, seem to sustain you in your earthly dream.

Beyond the dream, only the Love of God sustains you in reality for eternity.

You measure your self-worth and security by how little or how much money you seem to have. You hoard money in the belief that your security lies within its accumulation. Money will never establish your true worth. Only your willingness to give your mind to the Holy Spirit will allow you to recognize your Real Worth.

When you allow Holy Spirit to guide you, everything you need is given and you experience the infinite abundance that the Holy Spirit reminds the Son of God is his true inheritance. Put your mind and money in the service of the Holy Spirit and you will find yourself at peace, you will find you have made the decision to be truly helpful.

Your thoughts about money are merely a reflection of a fearful or loving thought. You know when you have not chosen love. You cannot escape the consciousness that God has created for you within. You need only listen as you make any type of exchange, and you will instantly know by the way it feels, whether or not the transaction was made on holy ground, or darkened ground. Should you notice a sense of selfishness or unequalness, you should then stop, and ask within for my help, allowing the Holy Spirit to decide for you how to proceed.

If you experience a sense of unity and joy between you and whoever you are dealing with, then you can be assured that you have decided for joy, unity and fair celebration with everyone involved.

Where the Presence of spirit is absent there can be no real sharing, no real joy. If you have decided alone in any decision that should involve every party involved, then you have sold out to fear. The result is a guilty sensation for anyone, because guilt is the result of deciding without love and all alone.

Before making any money transaction, always decide with the help of the Holy Spirit. I wait with the Holy Spirit to help assist you in your guiltless decision to become truly helpful. It is never hard to decide in any decision where you do not perceive separate interests. No hardship awaits any one who has asked God first and then waited for His Holy Decision for both of you.

Remember this: you are one with every brother and sister you meet. When you decide, you decide for both of you always. There is never any decision that you can make that does not involve more than one person! Everyone is affected by whatever decision you may make. Remember this always, and you will always decide together and righteously so.

Never let the ego decide for only one. When you allow your mind to decide for one and not all, you are giving way to the ego's temptations, and, you are deceiving both yourself and all your brothers and sisters. You never deceive merely one.

Since you are joined in Christ as one Self, any decision effects not one, but the whole son-ship. This is how you will remember your One Self: by asking for His Help with every decision you make. His Decision will always be inclusive, just as God included everyone as part of Himself.

Your decisions are for all or for no one. For if you merely decide selfishly, you have made no real decision at all. Any decision that is not inclusive is illusory and is wasted. All forms of exclusion are delusions, and are therefore not true and have no meaning or value.

Listen then, and ask for the right decision to be made by the Holy Spirit for you. You indeed will know when you have decided correctly, for His Decision brings only true joy and complete peace. If you experience this after making a decision with the guidance of the Holy Spirit, you shall know yourself and your brother and sister by the fruits you have shared.

God will never fail you in bringing to you a complete sense of freedom upon your choice to ask first. And Christ will be in both your heart and mind upon your simple decision to ask and then proceed as the loving Answer is given.

ON

CAREER

You all often confuse making money with what you refer to as your "careers."

Employment and making money are transient. Whereas your true career is a lasting reflection of the personal journey you have agreed to take and learn from while living in the illusory world.

A career may involve making money, and it may not. There are those of you who make no distinction between the two and are able to find joy in the process. There are also those of you who need to make the distinction between the two, and either way is okay.

There is no judgment on God's part as to how you find your joy. It may be career related or it may not. Some may have occupations that they really don't care for, yet they do it because this is what they need for now. Others may make clear distinction between employment and careers.

However, it is best that everyone can, at some point, not make a distinction between employment and careers, for they have remembered enough of Heaven to realize that enlightenment can be experienced in everything you take part in.

Clearly, the road with no distinction is one of more graciousness as well as simplicity, and it reflects an attitude that is stable and certain in every place they find themselves in. You need not get paid to be truly helpful.

Yet there is no shame or deceit in receiving pay for being truly helpful. Some feel great integrity by not making this separation. Others feel the need to make a clear distinction. There are no rules, except that the goal of any effort should be the experience of joining and joy. In this world it can be difficult to find joy in performing the skills required for employment. Although the goal of mankind should reflect a bridging of this gap, so that through social evolvement each one learns together that joy can be experienced anywhere and at anytime.

Remember, we are always on the path of remembering God together. This calls for clear and loving communication, with integrity that defines no gaps or distances. The spirit of God is everywhere at all times, because there is no time or distance between what is truly created.

It is clear that a selfish desire to "get" is an obstacle that causes a sense of separation between two or more people. This causes a break in communication that can indeed be called "time." Yet time is illusion, and not reality. The experience of timelessness is everywhere, and within an instant that is immeasurable by physical means.

The purpose of your entire journey while seemingly living in the world is to escape these breaks and detours. It is as simple as being determined to become truly conscious of love in all activities, no matter how big or small. You may be making change at a cash register, and a stranger's glancing smile may suddenly awaken you both to the joined state of heart and mind that created as your One Self.

The most difficult parts of your life can therefore be changed by the different view that you are here to join with everyone, and not to act in ways that precipitate the opposite effect. This change of mind is the miracle.

The idea is to put enough of these mind shifts in line so that your perception becomes of desire for true vision and not the opposite. This is why an offering of love and forgiveness without expectation is the means to escape the darkened dreams of time and to remember Who indeed you truly are, and, what you truly share together.

There is no miracle in an act as simple as receiving your change at a grocery store, unless you give your judgment up of the act as it occurs. This we call being conscious of the Holy Instant, a spiritual state that is always present and always freeing for everyone who chooses to remember what is truly significant in that instant. This takes effort, but only the effort to overlook the ego's agenda and envision Heaven in that instant you are always given to share with whomever.

You can in your Oneness achieve a major shift on a planetary scale if you join together in purpose. For the miraculous mind is for everyone without exception! Allow light to heal through you, become truly helpful in whatever occupation you serve through. Bring real compassion and true helpfulness with you to work as well as play.

Commit to this compassionate lifestyle first without exception and by this you will remember the true purpose for everyone and help each other to find it. Genuine healing begins with your decision to place forgiving gentleness first in all situations. It is not complex, but truly simple, yet your own thinking has taught you to replace this with fear and survival thinking, which no longer works.

This may be described as an overlooking of whatever particular agenda the ego has in mind while seemingly passing in time. You need to look past time to experience your shared Treasure. Everyone waits for you to do this. Your brother and sister are counting on the next person they meet to help them with this change of mind.

And it is always you whom they look to, to remember God and Heaven with.

Your "career" is but another masked preoccupation without your conscious decision to win more from the very situation you are experiencing right now. The carpet of time is but the same illusion rolled out which seems to have depth and distance. It does not! Your chance to better your career, your life and all of your relationships depend on how conscious and centered on the love you share right now.

There is not one of you who does not want this true and all encompassing love and quiet compassion. It is the whisper of a swallow's wings while in flight, the sound of the trees gently blowing in the wind, the sun reflecting warmly off the pink cheeks of a beloved child. It is what you came here to remember. It is all you ever wanted or ever will want. It is the desire to be at home with all you love and all who love you. It is the note-less sound of Heaven, the gurgle of your favorite stream in the woods. It is this quiet Home which calls to you.

And in every occupation you may pursue, it is the reflection of Heaven and its shared joy you hope to find. Look carefully and gently with your sisters and brothers little child. I stand peacefully between you both holding both your hands.

The path is clear. The discovery of Heaven together is your real occupation. And in each instant that passes, there it is—another opportunity to discover the great and peaceful light of Heaven together. We are joined on this journey together brother and sister, for without you it cannot be found. Together can we now share what is only created for us both, together now, here in Heaven. In whatever you choose to do, choose together and with wings of light and helpfulness to all. This is the way the world works to remember Heaven!

ON

FEAR, GUILT AND ANGER

Let us speak frankly about fear, guilt and anger.

From fear comes guilt and from guilt, anger, blame and attack. The correction of all of these comes when Love is remembered. Whenever you are afraid it is because you believe you have lost something: be it your safety, sanity or a person or thing. Loss always makes you feel angry and guilty if you believe in it.

Yet, I am teaching you to question this belief. It might be as simple as reminding you that you came here with nothing but love and you will leave here with nothing but love. However, the ego would always argue in favor of keeping your anger and blame, teaching always that it will get you something.

You do not need anger, blame and guilt to keep your life in order. All of these emotions are forms of a kind of hatred. And hatred, made entirely of delusion, is the foundation of the ego and thus the world as you see it. You see the world as trying to take something from you. You see the world as vengeful. You see the world as merciless and untiring in its quest for your sanity. Yet when you no longer choose the world, you will awaken in peace.

The core of the ego's thought system is based in its hatred for God. For the ego truly believes that God cast it down from Heaven, and that it is now up to it to "save" you. Yet let us look carefully at how it would "save" you.

The ego truly believes that you are separate from both God and your brothers and sisters. In its sight you are both merely bodies, destined for death and destruction at some unexpected time, perhaps delayed awhile, perhaps soon, but none the less, inevitable. The ego's response: protect the body while shutting out God and love.

The very part of your mind that would gently remind you that you are indeed safe is thus hidden from you. The ego believes that by protecting anger it can insure its proclivity, and on this point alone it is correct. Yet you must learn to ask yourself honestly, "Is this how God would want me behave?"

The ego would teach you that you are inherently bad, and therefore deserving of guilt, and thus, anger. The ego further believes that by punishing you somehow, it can exonerate itself from its feelings of inadequacy and hatred. Yet, given a careful look, this makes no sense. For punishment is how the ego maintains the trick of its existence. Through the laws of punishment, the ego is made to feel "alive," while spirit is merely shelved and forgotten.

The idea of punishment is always a projection of hatred onto another or yourself. Through the idea of punishment, the ego is able to maintain its hatred, thus building the illusion of its grandeur. But the ego can never be anything but very small. So tiny, in fact, God does not even recognize its little existence. And here the insane idea that you can exist apart from God must come into question. Would God ever punish His own Son and Daughter?

You cannot be punished except by you, through your own thinking. No person can ever take from you what you are in God who created you. Nor have your own ideas on self-debasement ever really hurt you. Nothing you can do or say can take away from your creation, which is established and maintained by God forever.

Thus, anger, fear and guilt have no purpose in Heaven or under Heaven, except to maintain the trick of the ego's existence. Yet I have said you do not need the ego to have an ordered lifestyle. For everything good that has come to you has been given to you by God. And everything that has seemed to hurt you or keep you frightened was offered by the ego. Do not accept any "gifts" it would offer to you, and remember that only God's love is without condition.

ON
RELIGION
AND THE
BIBLE

Many interpretations of the Bible have viewed God as one who both condemns and forgives, but I assure you that He does neither.

Any interpretation of the Bible that is other than a loving one is, indeed, in error. The battles fought for God in its stories are utterly meaningless unless they can be interpreted as calls for love. The different punishments that God was said to have called forth upon some of His sons are simply untrue. God nevr condemns. The ego, however, is liable to condemn you or others any time it is unhappy about how it sees a turn of events.

It is not necessary for you to read the Bible or any other religious book in order for you to remember God and know that He is with you always. In fact, a slight turning away from both dogma and perception is necessary to experience any degree of enlightenment while living in this world.

God is spirit and so are you. What you are is therefore beyond perception and interpretation, and remains stable only in creation. Love is your creation. It is not open to the question of perception. Your thinking is therefore unnecessary in regard to your own experience of God's Knowledge and Love.

How well you are able to still your own mind and stop thinking is the measure of how much you will be able to truly experience your Self in God. And you may note that a very few have been able to still their minds to any lasting degree. However, it is through this stillness that God will soon speak to you. He may speak to you in words or feelings of joy, depending on which you can more easily accept at the time. But speak He will.

When you are truly experiencing joy, you will not need these words or your own to hear. Hearing the Word of God is both spontaneous and joyous in recognition that the world you are seeing is not real. It is the letting go of your own perceptions that will reunite you with God. When you no longer take this world seriously, God will gently replace it with His joyous World of Heaven in you.

Is there anything that you can do to bring about experiencing more closeness to God? Of course! You can learn to unlearn trust in your own perceptions. You can learn not to take your own perceptions seriously, but instead, take love and spirit most sincerely. You who are lost in a world of perception and illusion can hardly doubt the importance of such an achievement!

You can learn by unlearning to see outward, and then, experience love inward and everywhere. Remember, it is your thinking that got you right where you see yourself. It is the removal of this thinking that will one day reunite you with your Father in Heaven. But do not underestimate your own thinking. Your thinking is your religion apart from God!

The religions of the world are, for the most part, based on separation from each other and God. Remember that interpretation is not fact, and every religion is based on interpretation. Even my own words since the crucifixion have been altered, changed and made by religion to appear as something they are not. I am not angry because of this, but many others have become angered through their interpretations that God is both angry and condemning. Let me remind you that you made hatred, not God.

The evolvement of the human race depends much on the letting go of hatred and anger. Hatred robs each of you of your natural talent for helping and assisting others, a condition which will soon become necessary for the whole of humanity to continue. The competitive ways of getting, arguing, fighting, outlawing, imprisoning, dealing and stealing must soon be replaced by sharing, forgiveness and giving. If this advice is not soon heeded, religion and government will be shown to have failed you miserably.

And upon this recognition, slowly but surely, you will all begin to truly awaken to the necessary truth: the fact that you are all truly one, not as a metaphor, but as a reality. And to live together in God means to forgive and help, not in a few cases, but in all. Remember this: punishment is never helpful or justified.

ON
EVIL
AND SATAN

Look at the ways in which the world seeks to fix, change, control, manipulate and punish others.

All you need do is look around you and observe. Notice in the world how getting is placed foremost in front of sharing, giving and forgiving? Many of you are now living dreams of unforgiveness. An example of this is to say, "Every one for themselves"; or, "He who has more wins." Be honest. Have you not been trained to believe that getting is a greater goal than sharing? It is this dream that we must somehow shatter. Your waking up depends on it.

If ever there was evil or Satan, it is in the act of getting and taking. Hoarding is the most dangerous act committed in this world. It has closed you off from those who truly need help and left you in your own cold and darkened closet, beyond the reach of God's light and love. You do not realize what you have done to yourselves by not sharing, for you have cut yourselves off from your own loving hearts. And this, dear ones, is indeed tragic!

When you refuse to share you are making a statement that you believe that you are all alone in this world. And you will live your lives as if you are alone. Sharing is an act that God committed when He created you. By sharing His spirit with you He gave to you life. But you do not recognize this eternal life unless you share it as He does.

You should not so much give of your money and your possessions as you should give of your compassion, joy and understanding. By listening to others you are giving a great gift of love to them and yourself. Evil is the opposite of giving, and of listening. When you do not listen you are apt to act out of fear and not love. This not only closes you off from spirit, but also closes you off from each brother and sister who waits to share with you. Sharing comes from God who created you by sharing.

You who do not share should fear the "god of evil" whom you made to keep you separate from all others. By not sharing this is what you have asked for. And so you shall receive as you have asked. Your god may not be real, but since you have asked for him you will believe he is real.

When someone refuses to share with you, do not be quick to point it out, but instead, overlook their error by offering to share something with them. Error is never corrected with another error. And you should learn that all error is corrected by sharing peace with each other.

There truly is no evil or Satan. You have made him true for you only by withholding love from one another. If another commits an act of aggression against you, how can you correct his error by terrorizing him as well? You can be hurt by him only by accepting his error of aggression as "true," and you need not do this unless you believe that both of you have been abandoned by God. God could never abandon you, but you can abandon Him temporarily by holding on to your own errors of lack and attack.

You seem to experience evil because you believe evil is possible. Yet if everyone knew for sure that God never abandons them, even in "death," where is evil then? Evil is thus a form of your own fear of death. It tries to convince you that you must get while you can, and hold onto whatever you have. Yet what part of the world will you take with you when it is time to lay your body down and return home to God?

If even for a moment you can live your life as if you had already died you will remember Heaven. If all that you have gained in this world has already been given up willingly in your heart, you will remember what you are and from Where you came. And if death is recognized as unreal, where is Satan and evil then? Now you will surely know that nothing can be taken from you, but only increased by your giving.

ON
SUPERSTITION
AND MAGIC

Magic is the belief that something from outside the body can be taken for healing purposes.

Superstition would teach you that certain extreme rituals and idols can be healing or damning. Miracles, on the other hand, teach you that only by remembering spirit can you be truly healed. Magic fixes the problem temporarily, while miracles abolish the problem completely. Some of you are afraid to utilize miracles for healing. And for this, magic can temporarily be used. Realize however, that magic is only temporary, and can hold you back on your quest for true spiritual understanding and healing.

There are many forms of spells from which a society suffers. The belief in taking a substance for healing purposes is one of them. Yet it stands to reason that if an illness has a sufficient hold in your mind, it may be better to depend on outside cures temporarily until the mind can be returned to the sanity of love.

The world now suffers greatly from the belief in magic, medicine and superstition, all of which are forms of spells. By taking something from the outside to heal, you are at the same time believing that your mind is weak. However, it does not figure that you should give up your dependency on magic when you feel weakened. The mind that is weak needs something else to believe in temporarily. In this case medication from the outside should be a viable option.

Understand however, that your mind is the strongest force in the universe. Within you is God. And you can move mountains either in front of you or away from you with this power. The ego will always tell you to depend on some thing to heal or become happy. But remember that "going shopping," taking a pill or finding a new boyfriend are temporary. A true healing must still take place at some point. And this means that a denial of the material and an affirmation of Love are at some point necessary.

Healing is never physical and always emotional. Physical healing, if it is to take effect, always results from emotional healing first. Since all healing is truly emotional, it now makes sense that you look within you first for answers. If this isn't sufficient for a healing, then ask from without for help.

By approaching healing in this manner you will apply first the power of your own mind connected with Gods to heal. Then if you still feel you must apply from without, you will not have forgotten the willingness to remember your own perfection first.

Remember always that nothing you take can correct a misplaced thought system. If your thinking is set to depend on the physical, you will automatically look outside yourself for help, thus reaffirming your belief in magic over and over.

At some point even the most physically dependent mind comes to realize the futility of its mistaken dependency, and begins to look inward again for an answer. It is up to you how long this will take. As I have said, you can greatly shorten the time it takes for healing by always looking within first. Then no matter what the decision your trust will first be where it belongs.

It can be said that illness can most often be equated to a willful mind and a weakened relationship to the heart of one's being. For a while most everyone experiences this to some degree, because the mind of the ego truly believes that safety lies within its own separate and unique ability. As the ability to "get" slowly comes into question, the mind can temporarily lose sight of a clear goal, thus leaving it vulnerable to some form of illness.

But as the mind remembers its true place in the heart, the place of giving and sharing instead of getting, then is strength more truly obtained and a foundation in the safety of Love made sure. As this occurs the dependency on the physical diminishes and spiritual sight increases, uniting one with all beings sentient or otherwise. Joy becomes the one factor that is sure with the one who has committed her mind to the heart of Love in all.

ON

SOCIETY
AND MASS
CONSCIOUSNESS

The views of a society are reflected by the weaknesses and strengths of individuals, either united or not united with others.

The greatest leaders are those who lead for peace and not war, for peace is what the world is lacking.

You may believe that the world is not at war, but you must ask yourselves sincerely this question: "What are the goals I place before my own peace and the peace of others?"

Ask yourself this question often. You may discover that all the goals of "getting" come before your own peace, and thus you suffer from your own inner war. Does not this inner war reflect into the world you seem to see and experience?

There are those of you who give to get, and this is indeed a goal that puts you out of harmony with God and your true Self. That which you attempt to sell to another you cannot share with her.

Giving to share and receive peace, on the other hand, is the loftiest goal you are capable of achieving. When you give without any conditions, no matter what the form, you are aligning your will with God's and the true will of every sister and brother.

ON
DISHONESTY

Dishonesty is always a form of denial, and indeed this is really what you are addressing here.

And it is also really what bothers you: the denial of Love. I have said before that lies eliminate themselves because only truth is truth. What seems difficult is not the fact that someone is blatantly telling you fantasies and stories; it is the realization that underneath you are both missing the Love you could be sharing. And this realization often prompts the uncovering of the repressed and outrageous belief that perhaps you could both be separate from God. A teacher has come; healing is in order.

JESUS, I WOULD LIKE TO ASK OF YOU THIS QUESTION: IF A PERSON IS BEING CONTINUALLY DISHONEST WITH ME (AND PROBABLY WITH HIMSELF), HOW CAN I TRUST THIS INDIVIDUAL AND WHAT HE SAYS TO ME?

Although the forms of dishonesty can be many, the foundation is always fear. By all appearances, however, a person may not seem fearful at all. He may come across as angry, manipulative, childish, spiteful, crafty, and the list goes on and on. The form does not matter. It is always a cover for the belief in scarcity, and thus the idea of littleness. And a fearful child may be dishonest, for somehow he must believe that his Power is not within him, but outside instead.

How can you trust in what he says to you? By simply trusting in what he really is (spirit), and not in trying to trust in what he is not (a body). His illusions are never true, and nor are the ones in you in which you think you see in him. His cover for littleness is also yours if you make it so. And this is what you choose each time you see his dishonesty instead of the inherent honesty you both share.

You see dishonesty as the untruth. And everything that you think, say and do is a lie because in its inherent incompleteness it cannot wholly represent the truth. And only in the truth do you experience God's peace.

You hate yourself for your own self-made misperception and picture of dishonesty. What you truly hate is your rejection of the truth through the partial picture that you made up. Thinking excludes knowledge and knowing, and therefore is only partial by the very perception it rests upon. Come to the truth in gentle silence to be healed.

Perception is always open to interpretation. God never interprets. Nor do you really need to once experience replaces symbolism. Symbols lead to or away from enlightenment. Enlightenment is an unspeakable instantaneous experience. It is complete in itself and remains indefinable.

That is what I have come here to offer to you. I accepted the light completely for all time, which is the truth. All dishonesty fell instantly away as it will for you. Give me your thoughts and let us join together in accepting the truth and receiving the truth, which is the love of God. You shall have the same experience that I now have always, and we will be joined in this constant and eternal light together. Your guilt will fall away and is replaced by what is already eternally created: the quiet and gentle truth of what you are.

You cannot accept and know the truth of what you are when you still hold the guilt of who you think you are. Release your past and guilty perception to me, and you will know yourself along with me. You will know me. And as you accept and know me, your Self, your brother and your Father will quietly shine as one as your joyous experience.

Frightened children feel a need to keep secrets, because what is hidden is believed to empower and get them more of what they want. And what they want is a Power they feel they have lost or do not possess. The ego will always be a frightened powerless little child, dear one.

And a frightened child can sometimes seem vicious and insane, for he has not learned to give the Gift of his own Inheritance, and so he does not know he has received it. Would you remind him that his little secret is a childish and weakened lie and make him more afraid? Or would you remind him instead of the truth that is already in him now by sharing only this of yourself? Learn then to overlook littleness, for it is illusion.

There is nothing of mistrust in him that your complete trust in Christ in you both would not instantly shine away in both of you. Your complete trust in the Self you share makes trust in this world unnecessary. For the world, its thoughts and all its deeds will never have their place in Heaven. And in your trust of only Christ in your brother and sister, the world through each of you will surely be forgiven and vanished. And where are lies where Christ's genuine compassion has come?

ON
LAWS
AND RULES

The laws and rules of society are made to protect the body, and surely no one would question this.

And so, the laws of men fall within the framework of the human ego as a physical part of the world. You need not necessarily challenge the laws, but instead, rise above the tendency to live your lives as if you have a need to be coerced by them.

Some laws are designed to protect the few instead of the many, and these laws are less than helpful, and could be looked upon carefully. When a law helps all others to recognize their own unlimited abilities instead of hindering them, then it allows for individual as well as social growth among equals. Laws should not be made to establish boundaries for punishment and to scare, but to provide all with ground-rule instruments to assist in providing an environment for peace.

If you are among those who choose to live their lives in a spiritual fashion, then you must seek to live without a sense of coercion. If you seem coerced by the laws of men, chances are good that you are failing yourself and your brothers and sisters regarding the ability to love and be loved.

Those who live for the peace of God need neither coercion nor the laws of men to guide them. You can choose to be guided by the laws of men, which are based in fear, or the laws of God, which are based in Love. If you would live your lives "in love" you will immediately transcend the seeming necessity for the laws of men and their effect on you, thereby unnoticing them. If you live a life of fear, chances are great that you will attract an application of man's laws into your life.

Remember that fear always entails the idea of getting and taking. The laws of men are also just that: the idea of getting even and taking away rights and freedom if you break them.

You need not be concerned with man's laws if you are one who is concerned with peace, sharing and giving. Nor should you be. And rules for living should be made along these premises. Those who break rules do not deserve punishment, but more understanding, help and compassion from those already living peacefully in God's Will. And remember this: the more rules and laws that you make, the more that will eventually be broken. Consider, then, what the making of too many laws and rules must have.

With an overabundance of your own laws and rules, there will be many more who will break them. And if you believe another has broken a law, then you will also assume she deserves whatever judgment is made towards her. Can you see the danger in this?

When a judgment of guilt is made and punishment of a sort is prescribed, you teach one another to accept that punishment from another or a society can be deserved, and that guilt and blame are equally deserved and are now inherent within the punishment prescribed.

But ask yourselves this: does God will for anyone guilt and punishment? The answer of course is "no." God could never will for anyone guilt or punishment because He created each of us entirely innocent of the ego's laws and treachery. The "hell" that seems "deserved" is also a fantasy of our own projected and unhealed hatred.

The question that all must ask as a society is this: What is the value in teaching anyone blame, guilt, punishment and hatred? And what will be the social consequences of our teaching this?

If prisons were kept for only those who were deemed violent or potentially violent offenders, then you wouldn't have to build more prisons. And with less people in prisons, less would also be learning how to hate and rebel more.

Why does this seem so difficult for politicians and lawmakers to understand? Or perhaps they do understand but choose to overlook it because of their own fears of not being well liked by the majority. These are the deeper questions that must be soon answered.

When forgiveness is replaced by grievances as a cornerstone to empowering government, what is to become of its people and the whole world around them?

ON
PUNISHMENT
AND
REHABILITATION

What if all of the prisons in the world were turned into rehabilitation centers, training inmates in socialization and educational skills?

Those doing life sentences would be voluntarily trained in teaching skills, their punishment for capital crimes would be to assist and to help others in prison the rest of their lives. They may never see a regular society again, but they could help teach and train others to live and love, in or out of society.

The idea here is this: every soul is truly redeemable. God knows it is this way. Why shouldn't society at least try and come closer to God's standards? We are born into this world to learn to help each other and thus remember Heaven together. Perhaps if we fail in our mission, we are given as many chances as are necessary to accomplish our true function here.

The experiences in life that seem painful are due to our failures in remembering that we are really in Heaven together, dreaming for awhile that we are living separately in this world we think we feel, see and touch. If there ever was an experience of hell, it is our thinking and our senses that bring it to us, not by the love that we share.

God gives us lifetimes of opportunities to heal, help others and awaken. We should honor each and every life, giving to each the same opportunity, no matter how dark and limited the circumstances may appear.

You may think it idealistic of me to suggest that we teach criminals and prisoners the ideas of helping and healing. But, are not these circumstances the exact circumstances that call the most for help and healing?

Perhaps by putting some people who have made mistakes and committed crimes into prisons we believe we have solved a problem. But what happens so often when a prisoner is released from a prison? They often repeat the same crimes and mistakes as they once did before. Our system fails to rehabilitate, often causing the parolee to repeat an offense, and even more intensely than before.

If we teach those who have wronged us through punishment and degradation, we only reinforce the same ideas that they started out with. Those of us who commit crimes have often been taught as children through punishment and degradation. How can we escape such ideas unless we are introduced to new ideas that are based instead in forgiveness and healing?

Any system of government that is based more strongly in punishment than in forgiveness is bound to backlash against a whole society. And who, then, is the greatest criminal, the system that taught the criminal, or, the actual criminal?

When we teach punishment in any form, we reinforce it within ourselves and in others. The result is a society that is bent on control rather than understanding and compassion. The idea of control complements the idea of punishment. In fact, control and punishment are ideas that live together side by side. Neither of these ideas really work. Why? Simply because these ideas are without love and compassion.

What happens when an adult tries to control a child? The child acts out, only worse each time, often later trying to counter control the situation. When a child tries to control his friends he quickly becomes friendless. No matter what age and circumstances, control and punishment never really work. The later effect being a rebellious society and a rebellious world.

The idea of punishment and control are signs of a diseased society. People are much more apt to respond to any situation in which love and compassion are being offered instead. You may believe you live in a world of opposites. This is not really true. Only love has ever really worked. The rest is but a dream, and this is what you refer to as the world. The question is, are you asleep dreaming of what you are not, or, are you awakening to what you truly are?

When you begin to awaken, it is because you have allowed the idea of rehabilitation to take the place of the ideas of punishment. You may believe this is a simple process. And it is. But it does not happen so quickly as awakening from your sleep at night. When one begins the process of spiritual awakening, it starts with the realization that you must be dreaming. Then, you may begin to dream that you are indeed awakening. And finally, you will awaken when the process of self-forgiveness is completed.

No one, however, can awaken while they still believe they are being punished, controlled or coerced. How much better it is to awaken from the dream of punishment and coercion by forgiving and helping others, and in releasing them from their own self-made prisons. No other way is there to be free. Your brother stands within the walls with you, or, outside the walls with you. But the decision begins with you and the choice you make.

ON
INSANITY

The term "insanity" can be safely used to define the human ego.

As we have discussed before, the ego always wants to get something. Its concern is therefore never on giving and sharing, at least without some sort of condition or expectation.

Those who seem insane are those who are most caught up in their beliefs and thoughts. They often see nothing beyond their own thinking, and believe that their thinking is indeed real.

You must learn to question the reality of your own thinking. The more seriously you take your own thoughts, the more you will approach experiencing the full meaning of insanity.

The closest your thoughts can come to sanity are through the ones that are loving. But looked at more carefully, a truly loving thought is not a thought at all. It is merely your true state of mind without thought of this world.

You who believe in insanity must find it difficult to believe and accept that you can live here without thought of this world. Yet not only is this possible, it is a necessary condition for your own salvation.

The fact is, you are saved from this world, and thus, you already live in the next, but without realizing it. You cannot comprehend the next world with your senses, but this does not mean it is not here.

It is only in the Holy Instant that you can experience the next world as here. For here and now is Heaven given to you and nowhere else.

That is why escape from insanity is as simple as changing your mind about what the world is for. You make the world you see and seem to experience by viewing yourself as a pawn or a victim of it. Whatever you seem to see must engender a sense of fear because your own seeing was made from fear.

That is also why nothing you see is really there, except in your own imagination. Your own thinking was made from fear and not from love. Even the loftiest thoughts you are capable of contain some element of fear. That is why you must learn to consciously and habitually exchange your thinking for the awareness of Love. You have learned so heavily to depend on your own thinking that, to you, to do without it seems insane.

I do not advocate that you should not have your own thoughts. Everyone who comes here makes a world for him or her self. The question is simply this: Do you want this world in light of what it has brought you?

If you are willing to give up your investment in it, another world will be given you in exchange. You will still experience your own separate thinking. But if you learn how not to take what you think or what others think seriously, together you can experience Heaven in the world's place. Is not the exchange of hell for Heaven worthy of you?

Do not underestimate the world you have made. It is clearly an attack on Heaven and God. For by replacing Heaven with your own world you have obliterated Heaven, and, at great cost.

Yet how easy it is to make this glad exchange! Heaven will come into you at your simple but willing invitation. You need not think of how, why or when. But merely make the decision to let your investment in your own sight go, and Heaven's grace will once again be shed onto you. How joyous the sound of a voice that is free. How light is the vision of those who would truly see!

ON
AUTHORITY
AND
JUDGMENT

The authority and judgment of a person is never true.

Either must contain some element of fear and doubt, and lack the full judgment that only God is capable of. You may believe it is okay to judge against hatred and violence. Yet look at what your own hatred and violence has done. You hate what seems violent, and violate and exclude those who would hate. You even exclude yourself from your own violent thinking, which you made only to protect an image of yourself. How, then, can you judge anyone or anything correctly?

You did not come here to learn how to judge for yourself, but instead, how to learn what it means not to judge. You are the author of insanity, but not of reality, which God created changeless for you, and therefore beyond your own judgment or the judgment of others.

Any authority that you have been endowed with may be true in the eyes of men, but is entirely false in the realm of God. Understood in this way, which I promise you is true, is it not easier to be and live as God created you?

Judgment and authority are both problems in the world you see, but not as God knows you. You need not make either of them your problem unless you insist on attempting to usurp God's Will.

Unless you are under the coercion of misjudgment and false authority you need not be concerned about God's Will, which would only release you from both. But if you are under this coercion you will feel less than you are capable, thus becoming egotistical in order to compensate for your own misperceived lack.

This has the effect of making you seem tyrannical instead of loving, thus leaving you to feel separate from others as well as God. Eventually everyone must give up the idea of being author or judge of anything, for only God is Author and Judge.

Child of God, you were created to create, not to author or judge. To create means to accept your own reality as you were created, and to allow the extension of this loving reality to others. The meek do not author, nor do they judge for themselves or others. Any enslavement of humankind is due to usurpation of judgment and false authority, both of which are merely delusional, and therefore, insane.

The one judgment that you can make that is correct is that you cannot judge. The one empowering and authorative decision you can make is never to decide for yourself alone. Instead, decide with God for everyone, without judgment or coercion.

ON
SPIRITUALITY

It is better to speak to you about your own spirituality than about your religion, because religion by definition is separatist, while spirituality is inclusive.

And because religion is separatist it imposes a condition of self-limitation based on its particular dogma or form. This does not mean that religion is "bad," but it does mean that it is exclusive in that if one does not agree with its particulars it tends to leave its non-believers outside its circle.

It is a misperception to assume that if a non-believer refuses to accept a particular religion that he will not be "saved." All of God's children are saved because of how they were created, not because of how they may think or by the rules of salvation they may at some point accept or not accept.

While religion sets out rules for how you should think and act, spirituality reminds you that you are under no laws and rules except for God's.

Quite simply, if you live and act lovingly you need no rules to follow because you automatically transcend all need of them. Those who become willing only to be truly helpful cannot be affected by laws, rules or tradition, simply because their full willingness to share all with all overcomes any need of them.

And this is how Christ will overcome the world: all its sin, pain, hurt and hatred will be simply left behind in glad exchange for the shared Heart and all of God's Love. What need have you of laws, dogma and rules who have risen above them all through total peace and harmony?

You may believe that it is idealistic to think that it is possible for mankind to transcend all its laws, but I would tell you that it is not only realistic, it is necessary for you all to evolve fully from your legal and political rules and ideals.

You who live in the world are like children who are growing up and learning to leave your limitations behind. Yet the limits you have made are there for you until you do. But your sharing with one another can greatly reduce the time involved for this full accomplishment to take place.

Every law of man that is broken is based within one delusional idea: the belief in lack. And how else can these laws be transcended except through giving?

Here is your spirituality made manifest to all, for by sharing you teach others of their own unlimited ability and potential. By giving without condition you expand the consciousness of Love and God to everyone, thereby blessing them and freeing them from the limitations and laws of the human ego.

If you are poor in body, rejoice that you are still indeed rich in spirit! And let spirit lead you to the abundance and freedom of your own inheritance. Begin by remembering what you are and from where you come. And as you rejoice in this remembrance offer it to all. And let all of the past no longer be there to deceive you, for you are rich now. Here is your joy.

Let this and every instant be a present reminder of your freedom forever! And keep it in your memory by sharing it with all. All that can be lost to you is not of God, and all that can be gained certainly is.

You who are spirit should know that you have everything, and you are everything. Nothing has been kept from you, for all is indeed yours. Let the present light in you be your guide to surety and safety. And let this Holy Spirit hold your joy and your peace for you by giving to Him all thoughts of fear, lack and guilt. You are an abundant, guiltless child of God. What limitations have you who are created in Him who loves you forever?

ON
EDUCATION

Education and freedom stand side by side, for without each other neither can be maintained or upheld.

The greatest student is the one who is filled with a sense of unlimited joy and awe. You can hardly offer either of these if you restrict someone through corporal or other punitive measures. Whenever you punish a child you induce him into either a depressed or hyperactive state, or, a vacillation between the two.

Learning is not accomplished through any kind of punishment, but through loving reward. Violence and depression are the natural outcome for those who are controlled, manipulated, punished or held captive.

You can even discover peace in the midst of a war zone; you can overcome the warring factor by learning to overlook the conflict in others, and by teaching them through your graceful attitude that control and punishment never work.

This is how peace will finally be brought to the world: by overlooking the seeming conflict entirely and offering only forgiveness, stillness and peace in its place.

In this world there are two kinds of education you can offer one another: spiritual education and material education. Each one of these naturally denies the need for the other because spirit is unattainable through any material means, and the world is disregarded with any recognition of spirit.

The world's education you learn through the use of your ego. Spirit's education is received through your unlearning of the world as a necessity for your own freedom. You can be educated in spirit as well as the world, but conflict will always arise unless you remember that only one is true.

The world you live in and interact in is the world of illusion. You are constantly making this world up in the way you alone choose to perceive it. That is why two people can so easily disagree about a particular perception.

With perception you imagine what you see and then make it real for you. However, with the acknowledgment of spirit there is no perception, and so everyone can agree with love.

Your educational system in the world is entirely out of balance because the focus is mostly on material education. Until the majority comes to realize the essentialness of spiritual education, the loss of peace and conflict cannot but continue. In fact, material education is not nearly as essential as spiritual education because spiritual education focuses on what is one and not on what is many.

The tendency of those who have learned to focus on the One is to not embark in disagreements about the many. Hence, it is necessary in completing the educational process to include principles of spirituality, without which the world becomes more and more conflicted.

It is not essential for you to necessarily instruct children on dogma and spiritual principles. All of the principles they need can easily be demonstrated to them within your own loving actions and decisions. Adults or children do not learn love through the action of teaching, but through the decision by you to demonstrate love in your own life. There is no compromise in this, and this is their real "education."

ON
COMMUNICATION

The law of communication is very simple: what is unloving is not real communication and, therefore, does not matter and does not really exist.

Everything truly communicative loves, and extends to everyone, everywhere. Your concern should not be with the unloving, which does not really exist, but with everything that is love and loving.

You and your sisters and brothers truly love whenever you leave your thoughts to me. You need not concern yourself with the seeming attacks of others, but merely with sharing with them what is not some form of attack.

Remember that when someone seems to attack you, you always attack yourself first. Change your mind about this and do not "buy" another's fear or hatred as your own. You cannot really share any form of fear or hatred because both are based in illusion and not reality, and therefore can never be shared or extended. Yet they can be comforted.

When you have remembered how to love anyone fully you will have offered love to everyone else simultaneously. This is because to love everyone truly is to love anyone fully.

Communication that is true is more often than not unsaid. Loving communication is taking place all the time, in every instant of every second in each minute, hour and day. You decide whether or not to be in touch with what communication is or isn't depending on which voice you choose to listen to.

Loving communication truly takes place without words and without thinking. The Thought of Love exudes through you and into your awareness and others when you clear a path in your thinking for it to do so.

You who seem to be in conflict are merely dreaming of war while standing in the very center of Heaven. You need not change the world or your position, but merely listen and awaken from the dream of your own separation.

Awakening reinstates your perfect Oneness with God and everyone now. Awakening lies beyond words and what can be thought, and lies in the realm of the experience of your own perfection.

When you listen only to what is on a person's mind you are cutting yourself off from your own heart and theirs. Emotionally, everyone who speaks is trying to share something with you from the heart. They may be calling for love or offering it to you, but they are always asking you to join God with them and for you both.

Ninety-nine percent of communication is listening, while the rest is speaking. That is why when you listen to your own mind you are not really listening, but interfering with communication. It is your thinking which got you into trouble, and only through your relinquishment of its vested reliance will you once again remember that you are indeed redeemed.

Child of God, you need not take yourself so seriously. In fact, it is better that you never do! Give your thoughts therefore to the Holy Spirit who will undo your investment in them. And thus they will fall gently away, giving way for the gentleness of Heaven to re-enter your heart and mind.

ON
TEACHING
AND
LEARNING

You are all teaching and learning each and every moment.

Yet the world's way of teaching is to instruct you to think. The Holy Spirit's way of teaching is to gently remind you that you need not think at all. Your thinking will always be there while you see yourself in the world, but you can remember foremost to depend on only one thought: the Thought of Love. The Thought of Love is God, your Self and your Life.

Teaching you to depend only on your own thinking is the ego's strategy, thus leading you blindly down a path of darkness, deceit and fear. You who would depend only on the ingenuity of the ego must lose touch with the genuineness and freedom which spirit would and could only offer.

God is not ingenious, but He is all-knowledgeable. When your will is at one with His and your mind is still, you become His Thought and only His Thought. This is why it is essential for you to stop thinking, so you can remember your real Home.

Remember the world and forget your own soul, or, remember your soul and forget the world. The latter may seem difficult, but I would remind you that you are never alone in the attempt to do so. The Holy Spirit will gladly accept any effort on your part in doing so, and will thus lift you quickly from hell back into Heaven.

Your part is so small it only requires a little willingness on your part. The little effort you make to not depend on your own thinking will be rewarded tenfold with His gentle but powerful reminder that you are indeed dwelling in Heaven.

You could easily awaken from your dreams of hell simply by allowing the light in you to come in and shine your dreams away. True learning is remembering the light through awakening from darkness. Yet if you insist on analyzing the darkness, the past and future, you place your mind in the grip of fear instead of love.

If you teach others to analyze with you, you are doing the same. Who but the insane would choose this at the cost of truth and salvation? The way of the world is to analyze everything, believing that without analysis all would be chaos. Yet look closely at the world and its present state. Is it not truly quite insane?

If you teach only love you will know only love. If you teach peace you will experience peace. If you forgive the world you must remember Heaven. How is it possible to teach only peace and live happily in the world? By trusting only in love to make every decision for you. With love's remembrance how easy the world becomes! And who would not look to the light in you to remember the light of salvation in themselves!

And yet demonstrating love to everyone you meet takes great dedication to the Holy Spirit and His Mission. The test can be great for those who deny the importance of the world in favor of love. Yet you have been chosen to accomplish just that.

Yes, little child, you came here to remember the truth for everyone. Would you not take the candle and lift it to every heart with me? For I am with you to help you join, serve and remember. Take my hand that we may offer our peace to the whole world together, and that each may remember our joining together with them. Our path is forgiveness. Our goal is God. Our return is most certainly unto Heaven.

ON

SELF-DISCOVERY
AND
EXPLORATION

The exploration of the self has been misunderstood ever since the invention of the ego and time began.

As we said before, the ego is an expert on invention and ingenuity, but a complete failure in all areas concerning the heart. To the ego, exploring its own inventions and lofty dialogues are what it sees as "self-discovery."

Your intellect is strongly devoted to the ego and its ways, leaving you blind to your own inner radiance and beauty. You believe that creativity belongs in the realm of invention.

The Holy Spirit knows, however, that true creativity belongs to the realm of spirit, or, the remembrance of what is already yours. True creativity is not gained or lost in you. It is simply remembered and then joyously shared.

Through offering miracles to others can you remember what you are with them. Inventions and magic, though temporary, can be exciting, but only miracles are truly illuminating, enlightening and lasting. Whatever the gift you offer, you offer to yourself first. And you will always receive it just as you have offered it.

You are not here to create the fallible, but to remember the eternal. The eternal is all you own, all that is yours and all that can be shared.

You can offer Heaven to a brother or sister just as easily as you can offer them the world. Which do you believe your sister and brother would really prefer? Each and every second you are offering them the choice of sharing with them Heaven or hell, light or darkness, love or fear.

But remember, what you offer them you offer yourself first, and then you receive the gift as your own.

The mind is like a conduit; it will attract whatever it is sent for, and likewise attempt to share it. Guard your thinking carefully and be aware of the message you are offering. It is always one of acceptance or denial. And then ask yourself, "Is this message worthy of sharing?"

Self-awakening cannot be undertaken by only you. Because of the way in which you were created, your real Self must be shared, or, extended for you to realize your own divine completion.

Upon your awakening you will no longer wish to remember the world, its things and bodies. All will but disappear in but the twinkling of an eye. And you will look upon the world as but a dream you have awakened from. And you will smile as everyone smiles with you. For they will see only what you see: the spirit of love everywhere.

There will be no more complexity and no more misunderstandings. You will remember that you are One with everyone. And there will be the quiet singing of angels all around you, lifting you on high into Heaven. Gently now, can you hear the angels sing to you to return with them?

ON
TECHNOLOGY
AND
INVENTION

There is one benefit to technology and invention: communication.

Without communication the joy of creation could not be remembered. Yet look carefully at what the majority of technology and invention are now used for. These inventions can easily be made to distract you from real communication. You do not realize the high percentage of time you are distracted from your own creation and natural humanity.

In the Bible this is the meaning of "the devil." What you call "the devil" is really the loss of touch with your own hearts. When you forget what is loving you are doing the "devil's" work. You cannot be truly joyous while you are distracted with what is obviously fearful. If you are to overcome "the devil" you must do your work with absolute and unconditional love in your hearts.

And you can do this merely by remembering that the world is but a dream and nothing more. Its complexity is meaningless in Heaven and so it should be meaningless to you.

You are all dreaming the world together. And so you must at some point choose to awaken from the dream together. Your only responsibility is to awaken first. Learn how not to take your dreaming, or the dreams of others, seriously.

Ingenuity is the misuse of your own creative ability. This applies to you. God will overcome the world when ingenuity is gladly exchanged for simplicity. Then will peace replace conflict. Few of you guard your own peace carefully enough. You often allow ingenuity to take the place of peace by allowing the ego to make decisions for you.

What you decide without love must be unloving. This separates you from your sisters and brothers and makes you good at business but not so good at sharing and becoming truly helpful. Thus, you are not living, but becoming the living dead. You have forgotten the loving Self God gave you in your own creation. He does not wish this for you, but you have, and so it is granted as you have asked.

Yet His Will for you will always be peace. And peace must be shared to be understood and lived. If technology must be used, use it only to bring the will of peace to all. Peace is true communication, and forgiveness paves the way to real peace.

Inventions and technology can all be used in the spirit of love. But they endanger this ability when they are merely used for self-gain and control. When "giving to have" finally replaces the idea of "giving to get" the world will have taken a giant step in spiritual evolution. When it is realized that having is giving and not getting, Heaven will be remembered on a widened scale. And this will bring in a new age for everyone.

One day you will all look back in wonderment at how you ever made it through the years of darkness when free sharing was more the unusual than the usual. Right now it seems unbelievable that another way of living is possible. But one day you will all wonder how you could have ever lived the old way for so long! My message to you now: help each other without conditions by comforting your souls.

ON
BUSINESS
AND POLITICS

God did not create you to ever be lonely.

Yet in the business of the world you are lonely. You need the Holy Spirit to lift you above and beyond its troubles and woes, and to gently remind you that you are not your business.

Nor are you the world, for the world does not really exist except in thinking that is unloving and faulty, and therefore it does not really exist at all.

Business and politics are both illusions of the human condition. But each may be overcome through the will to only share and love. You can each do truly helpful business by learning to be spiritually political.

By learning to truly serve without conditions rather than to merely take, and by remembering that ultimately, the goal of all business and politics is to remember how to express and share love with each other.

The reason there is so much darkness around business and politics is because the focus is so strong on getting and taking. This is an unhelpful form of communication. Yet it can easily be changed to one of sharing and giving once clearly understood that in this way it is helpful to everyone.

Herein lies the answer to your business and political problems: by applying spiritual principles to everyone you work or play with, business and politics can be unifying rather than separating.

The answer lies once again in sharing and not holding, giving and not merely taking. In this way business and politics can be joyous, rather than wearying you and those you work with. In this way business can be fun, and joy will be its outcome.

ON
RACISM AND PREJUDICE

The foundation of every conflict is based in some form of prejudice against something you think you see outside you.

Yet there is nothing outside you. You make the world and everyone in it just as you would have them be. It is your judgment alone that makes the world and everyone in it as they are to you.

Yet the world is nothing. And everyone else in it is love, just as you are. The fact that you do not see everyone as a part of love is obvious: you do not see yourself as love and as only loving.

You see the world as judgmental because you are judging the world. You see the world as hateful because you hate the world. If you take your judgment off the world the world becomes a neutral place, and suddenly everything becomes lighter.

The power of your mind has the ability for both self-destructive thinking and for complete renewal. It also has the ability to not think at all, but merely to receive and extend love. In this state you are at your best. While constantly thinking, you are at your worst.

The real question you must answer is: do you really want peace over conflict, or conflict over peace? There are those of you who do prefer the latter, and who even become addicted to it.

Imagine a state of mind in which you perceive only light in everyone you meet. A state in which all judgment of what or who seems outside you is not made at all. You believe that only God could perceive this way. Yet it is given you to perceive exactly as He does, for He created you for this.

I have said before that there is nothing outside you that you do not first see inside you. This is not suggestive. It is fact. This being the case it behooves you not to judge others since you always first judge yourself. You cannot hate anyone or anything without first hating what you see inside you projected out. And if nothing is really outside you then, there is nothing to judge but yourself. How, then, can you count on your own judgment except to confuse you further?

Racism and prejudice are both concepts of fear and not love. Both of these concepts are faulty to their core and therefore do not mean anything. It is arguable that if one projects hatred towards you, you should indeed return the anger and attack as a defense.

Yet consider this: in joining another in anger and fear you are merely locking both your minds from salvation. Where one wins the war and the other loses, both have lost in their ability to heal and be happy.

Racism and prejudice are at the core of the ego's insane thought system. Remove these two elements and the ego would be no more. Perhaps you do not realize how essential this understanding is for you to ever experience peace in this world.

Without realizing how completely insane these two ideas are you would be compelled to live by their codes. Yet when you truly consider what these beliefs do to your own ability to experience peace and feel happiness, only the truly insane would dare to hang on to these ideas.

Racism and prejudice can set the human race back to a state of mind beneath the animals. You do not want it. Therefore, do not uphold these concepts in any form or fashion.

Be vigilant for unity, love and God in everyone you see no matter how dark another may seem to you. Your light will help to pull him out of his darkened dreams of anger and fear.

Your brother and sister call to you for your light. Each seeks salvation with you, even though their demonstration may appear to oppose this.

Everyone wants love although they may demonstrate otherwise when they are afraid. Help your brother and sister to not live in fear by bringing to them the light in both of you.

Through your vigilant efforts, together you may help erase prejudice and racism in your lifetime, so Heaven will be reborn to you on earth. It is not evolution that will return you to your Home. It is the relinquishment of all that would attack or hurt another.

Since September 11th 2001, something extraordinary has been happening. Your prayers and your healings have been greater and stronger than ever before. The focus should not be on the war on terrorism that was started soon after the bombing, but on the joining and great healing that is taking place as a result. The terrorists were certainly unloving, but as difficult as this may be to hear, they have given the world a gift: the gift of rejoining and reuniting. Do not let this gift slip through your fingers!

On that day your seeming loss was felt in Heaven. And God holds each one who perished in His Arms, soothing each and reminding them that their families and loved ones have not left them. In their hearts they are each still with you, as you are all with them. And in your hearts, if you will be still and listen, those loved ones will speak dearly to you who feel such loss. Each one has not died, but truly lives on with each and all of your souls.

ON
KILLING
AND WAR

No one would question that killing and war are the unhappy outcomes of minds that believe them both to be a means to an end.

But in the case of destruction of a race or of another are the means ever necessary? I will tell you that they are not, but this will hardly convince you, because within your own thought system the justification for hatred and murder still exists, and will continue to exist until such a time that it is proven beyond a shadow of doubt that the outcome of such acts are truly only regressive and a misuse of time.

Killing, war, the death penalty and genocide are all merely ego justifications regarding your own belief in an inherent hatred and guilt. Your belief in any of these forms of punishment, that is, destruction of the body with whatever method may be acted out, is merely a reflection of your own beliefs in the plausibility of destruction of the self as a body.

Death is now feared to be "real" to you who believe in this in any of its forms. You now believe that death is a punishment for those bodies that have lived poorly, as well as for those who in your judgment have lived well, thus death is to be avoided at all cost and in any way possible.

Your belief in death is merely a projection of your underlying belief that you are vulnerable. Yet what you are is invulnerable to every kind of attack.

You could not believe in any of these forms unless in some way your faith in your own creation had somehow suffered. If you trust in God's eternal Heaven you could hardly decide to kill another, no matter what the circumstances were. It would merely be seen as a misuse of time, which it surely is, only making necessary repeated lives and lessons.

There is no death, but only reconciliation unto life. For many of you, many lives will be lived only to finally realize this fact. God is not dead, and so, never shall you be. You came here to remember exactly this. For life is not your body, but rather your heart and soul.

By killing or destroying another's body before their time you are only prolonging the inevitable, possibly theirs, as well as your own awakening to the realization of your shared eternal creation. For what does killing and war accomplish when it is realized it merely slows and hinders your own primal and spiritual awakening?

Those who would justify attack in any form will receive the same for themselves, by their own hand or the hand of another. For when you attack another you attack yourself first. But you also invite attack from another by attempting to make it real for both of you. It is never real in any form it may appear or seem to take, for attack in any form can never really hurt what you are. War, therefore, is not really to kill, but to scare.

You, whether as an individual or a nation, who pursue attack on others, are merely condemning yourselves to the fear of being attacked in return. And fear invites attack, as love invites defenselessness. This should be taught to all as a worthy state of mind.

Now, let us speak further about war. For war is about hatred, and hatred is inevitable to those who believe they are separate from God and from one another. War is merely a form of justified hatred and prejudice and nothing more. Yet what can be justified with happy and fair results for everyone except forgiveness and love?

It is natural for an animal to respond viciously when it or its young are attacked, but then it goes its own way, forgetting about its past confrontation. If a war ever must be waged it need not be justified, but completed quickly, without imposition on the aggressor, and in whatever form it needs to be complete, to join again in love and friendship.

No one would argue that war and killing another is perhaps the darkest of all human dilemmas from a human point of view. No one would argue that he who incites a war is *not* living a life in the light of Love.

Those who start wars always have ulterior motives. And a "good" politician always cites his or her motive as a product of "higher caring," without true regard to the real cause or motivation (projecting blame and achieving some form of selfish and unshared control). These you call your best politicians. For they are apt to get away with these incredible acts while making others believe in their mask of destruction called "peace keeping." There is no doubt that in every war begun only the lowest bidder hears about the "cost for peace."

War is never about bringing peace, but about achieving control and the appearance of autonomy of something and someone. It is a mad delusion that cannot be viably shared or truly understood at the time. It is madness and attack. And yet, it is nothing, for it means nothing. The value of war is, at best, the unmitigated delusion of theft.

You will all leave this world one day. And you will go together. Not by war and by killing, but by a simple loving decision to truly remember God together. The world is but a picture of deceit, darkness and corruption, a selfish place, where only the mightiest with their mightiest swords survive.

In this fearful dream you have all agreed to play your part in making the dream as real as possible. This is part of the unsaid agreement, hidden from view and having only the appearance of helpful nobility. You sit and watch the darkness, waiting to be swept away by yet another horrible atrocity. How will this situation be repaired? And so it seems ongoing.

You watch carefully, as if you were nurturing your own little child. You comment together on what you think you should do to escape from this nightmare. Yet nothing seems to work. And day-by-day this darkened picture-projection weaves itself deeper into your subconscious, changing each of your outlooks into slowly dimmed and continuous tainted movies of destruction and hatred.

Now you believe in mass consciousness, that some form of hatred from one side is justified, while scorning the other side, the side you have picked as your newest "enemy." All the while you believe that this enemy deserves whatever wrath the great politicians, the great "leaders" have sent upon them. You believe you need this darkened form of protection, this illusion that they will keep you safe from this dangerous hatred outside.

Little child, would you now remember that this darkness and attack only exists because you have interpreted it thus? These are your brothers and sisters. You who hold your God and religion so dear must realize that in only the relinquishment of all such sound doctrine will this lead you to the recognition of eternal Life. For any other interpretation of God and His Heaven must fall deeply short of His great omnipotence!

You see little child, it is but again a simple choice between eternal love and the illusion of hatred, darkness and fear!

God has no "way." He is the Way! There are no substitutes for true enlightenment. There is no need for you to worship my body or anyone else's. Love always rises above murder and injustice, above everybody in the world. There is no death, for what dies has never lived.

Yet how can anyone cling to the belief that death and darkness are justifiable, and all the more, real! Has God fallen short of creating His Son eternally? Is there exception to God's Law of eternal Life? Are some doomed by their crimes to be snuffed out altogether?

You who believe so should be sure that if your answer is yes, that you do, indeed, include yourself! For every one of you on your own have indeed murdered, if not alone or indirectly, together. Are you so willing now to condemn another when it is this, one hated brother who has turned the mirror back towards you? For it is him who reflects what you wish to see within.

You alone are asking for him to attack you whenever you choose to judge him as lesser or more unworthy than yourself or another. You ask for salvation in your prayers, but you offer to the one who sits next to you in need of help a form of veiled attack in the forms of judgment whom God and Heaven could never care of or know.

You came to the world to forget, now you have given yourselves no choice but to remember. And you indeed will, every one of you. But it is God who decides how this will be done. And for each of you who decide for yourself alone, you will not remember. You may try until you are ninety but you will fail miserably while you do it alone.

You cannot change God's Plan, and the more you insist that you can the more painful it must become. As time grows shorter and you grow wearier, the pain becomes sharper. Again, it is not God's choice, but yours and yours alone. You cannot make even the smallest decisions on your own and expect deliverance from hell. For hell can only be as small or as great as you wish it to be. And yet child of Love, 'tis is but a dream. Let God decide for you.

You may well ask, "If it is all only a dream what difference does it make what I do or who I help or hurt?" The difference, my child, is merely a question of whether you would rather continue sleeping and dreaming and never really knowing anything as God knows, or, awaken into the warm Light of Heaven and rejoice in eternal Perfection forever and ever! To minimize this choice would be quite foolish indeed. Now, it is merely very simple. Choose to no longer make the dream of life true, and reawaken in Heaven and never fear again.

You cannot bargain for a joyous Life. You are merely missing it because of your insistence in replacing it with your own selfish ideas of sanctuary. Be so glad your ideas have no validity! Be so glad that you have failed to make your own heaven. For if you had, there would be no escape. For behind the glitter and flowers is but a wall of darkness that leads to nowhere. You would be all alone in the universe had our Father not protected you from your own self-made devices!

Instead of trying so hard to take more of Heaven than your sister and brother has, change your mind! If you would know the garden, share then the flowers with everyone! There is nothing in this world worthy of Heaven. No amount of gold or money can bring to you peace of mind. In truth, every penny and everything you hoard is a waste of creative and healing energy. Not one thing you hold back for yourself will ever be truly helpful in your reconciliation with your brothers, sisters and God.

Yet all you give willingly and without a shred of reservation can but help you both remember together that this world and its things are but a dream! Escape from the dream with no conditions placed on your brothers or the world's things.

Truly you are only here to truly help. Could I be helping you if I do not share this truth with you? It could not be wise to ever place conditions on sharing the truth!

Sisters and brothers are being reborn to extract truth from their new experience where it was once withheld in the past. They are here to share love where once it was not possible.

Freedom of expression has not been present in every age. Yet these are the times of wonder and remembrance that time has no meaning or value. And then the need for the world will be quite over. For you will each remember that you have never been separate from one another or God. You will not value the thing you now cherish because you won't need them the way you seem to need them now.

Do you understand what I am saying little child? Your bad dreams are nearly over. All I need is what God needs: for you to give all of your fantasies and illusions up to Him who will exchange them for your own healing! Do not hold on to one last shred of your personal treasure. Do not allow any treasure to come between yourselves and God. I ask this from you as a savior and a brother. Leave the world behind and walk now with me to Heaven.

What if you each realized together that what has been valued once is now but an ancient and forgiven dream; a dream now made of only happiness and joy because nothing in the dream is longer held dear. Is this vision idealistic? Not if it is God's Idea! It is merely your Reality beyond all dreams.

ON

WORLD
GOVERNMENT

As the world unites, a world government comes closer to being realized.

This event is indeed some distance in time, but will surely come about one day, and the time can be shortened immensely through an adaptation to spiritual principles. There are still major lessons concerning separation for all the different governing factions to embrace.

For the most part, those who govern lack confidence in true conviction to a unified compassion and flexibility, reflecting sharply on the masses that allow these politicians to make strong decisions affecting everyone.

Politicians are far better at promising and threatening than they are at actually demonstrating, sharing and accomplishing. This is no fault of your own, for this seems to be a deeply learned behavior. But, this can rapidly change if introduced on an educational level.

The bottom line of any government, no matter how it appears, has always been "how much can we get and what will it cost?" This is simply standard business as it is now seen and experienced. A major distortion reminiscent in capitalism is that getting is far better than giving and sharing. This will someday change. And it must change for everyone in this world to truly experience a unifying solution.

The bottom line of a true religion is giving and sharing. The bottom line of a truly functional government is also the same. However, it does not make sense to approach this shift from a magnanimous point of view, but instead from an individual point of view.

Part of your own single spiritual evolvement requires learning to give and share without conditions. When you do this, you invite others to share equally in this process, inviting them to understand with you that enlightenment arises from sharing, not hoarding.

As a race, you will not approach reaching a world government until the above precepts are willingly put into use. Giving unconditionally to others is a precept to your own individual enlightenment. This may come in many forms, but whatever form of freely giving that you offer to others is a step towards truly uniting with others and God.

In retrospect, through history, by now you can easily see what the outcome of taking and stealing from others and other governments has offered you. Every war has been waged precisely for this reason.

Historically, God has patiently waited for all of you to remember that there is a better way: giving and sharing without your own sets of conditions. You probably even now respond to this message with a sense of disbelief. This is because you have not yet fully grasped the idea that there might well be a better way. Furthermore, you are even less likely to attempt to follow or adapt to it.

You are creatures of habit, dictated to mostly by your own fears and hatred. For all of you to transcend history you must overcome your tendency to lead your lives from past associations, ideas and learning.

Remember that every government is based on past learning. It's rules, laws and policies all stem from historical events. Can you see how this has clearly clouded your minds and hearts? Come out of the past, its crimes and hatred and anger, and live your lives in each new moment, free of fear and guilt from all past associations!

To do this is truly spiritual, and is what every true religion and path strives for. You all use so much time to bind yourselves to the past. You often live in what you call your closest relationships out of a sense of past clinging, locking you both into fear and unhappiness. This is far from spiritual! And yet your escape from this lies in unconditional giving instead of clinging. The clinging and conditions merely keep you each in fear and anger. This is hardly what you would want if you were thinking sanely and spiritually!

And so I say to you, adopt more policies of sharing and giving, and put away the policies dependent on taking and having. You will each know you truly have everything when you start to share it freely! And you will demonstrate to others by your actions that scarcity does not exist. Change your mind about just this and you will evolve in an instant to an awareness that normally takes you thousands of years!

ON
PERSONAL
PURPOSE

Your personal purpose is merely to allow healing for your own personal sense of separation from your Self, God and everyone, and then, discover eternal joy.

This sense of separation comes from your own unwillingness to allow it to be healed, being a form that you falsely identify with as your "self."

Naturally, you wish to protect what you see as your own private hell, a self that in no way resembles the truth about what you really are. The little self you think you see, yet take great efforts to hide, has been self-made from shame, darkness, fear and illusion.

Your sense of guilt and blame is all that keeps it "alive" in you. Your willingness to truly forgive the past is what removes all the limits you have upheld from your past mistakes.

You truly have nothing to identify with except the Love you are created from. Everything else is merely a dream of the ego's feeble making, an attempt at keeping your own belief in separation from Love real for you, a self-blame game. And out of this, an attempt to project the hatred you feel as a result onto others.

Yet you cannot hurl your anger and hatred onto another. By attempting to do so you only succeed in internalizing it and making it real for you. It is merely a disguised and displaced form of repeated self-blame.

It is much easier for you to get rather than to receive and give. You are apt to set up your own private kingdom in the world instead of preserving touch with your real Kingdom in Heaven.

Yet your own real personal purpose here is to allow whatever path you are taking to be turned into one of giving and sharing. You are so habitual about this one fact that it does little good to expose it to you, for you are used to insanity and are willing to "protect" it with your "life." Yet is this groping really your life you are living and protecting?

You protect illusions about yourself, little child, allowing the ego to separate your thinking from the peaceful truth. Yet without your thinking the quiet and gentle truth would indeed set you free as the One Thought it surely is.

How many have felt so secure in having a good job and a close relationship and then suddenly lost one or both, and then felt suddenly so lost and displaced? This is merely because they had set up their security in that which could fail them.

These are the great lessons you have come to learn here. And each will lead you closer to God if you will let them. If you do not, they will seem to lead you closer to "hell on earth," until you change your mind.

Your closeness to another is not established by the special conditions, expectations, hopes or goals you may place on another or hope to "share" with another. Closeness is not based in any kind of specialness. It is based in the holiness you each can truly share at any time, anywhere, at any instant, and, with anyone.

Your lack of imposing conditions will assist in helping you to remember your true abundance and Oneness with each other in the holy present. Remember always that with conditions comes blame, and where there is blame, a belief in guilt will surely follow.

Change your mind about placing conditions, blaming and accepting blame, for you are forever blameless and you are received wholly and unconditionally in the Eyes of God. So will you represent Him who sent you to all others, who are His children as well?

Your personal purpose of healing does not mean that you must live in one church. But let your church indeed be the whole world. Bring this church of love to every-one you meet by allowing it to shine in and through you to all He would have the light touch, excluding nothing or no one.

ON
TRUTH AND DECEPTION

Deception is always of the ego, which is built on lies.

When you deceive others you first deceive yourself. And not only do you deceive yourself, but unnaturally you begin to believe your deceptions are true.

Each of you has fabricated a self, which you believe is you. Indeed, this is what you have failed to forgive but need to forgive, so that you can remember your place and your power and take your place with those who have chosen Heaven in place of hell.

Truth is. You cannot alter it with your own lies or deceptions about yourself or others. And as much as many of you may wish to see yourself or others as un-whole you cannot change the fact that you and they have been created whole.

In order to deceive yourself or others you must first judge. It is always your own judgment that deceives you. This is why you cannot judge correctly. Only the Holy Spirit's Judgment is correct, and it is already made, being a part of the perfect spirit that created you.

Let us look, then, at what it takes to not judge for yourself so that you might remember your Self. Humility and arrogance are opposites, yet the humble see no opposites because they choose not to judge for themselves.

The cause of all your thinking comes from the coercion of what you believe is good judgment. Yet true good judgment requires no judgment at all. You may think it impossible to act without your own judgment, but this is not true.

Good judgment offers only healing action without your own judgment, relying on the Holy Spirit's instead. When you listen to the Holy Spirit's Judgment you need not judge at all. Nor will you be acting alone because the Holy Spirit is guiding you in each of your decisions.

When you have learned to judge with only the Holy Spirit you will also have learned how to only judge with others as well.

Truth always stands by itself. Deception stands only on faltering pedestals and will always fail you in the end. Deception is not a part of you unless you make it so. Truth will always be with you because you are the truth.

But you can choose not to listen to what you really are. Therefore, give up all lies and deception about yourself and others and awaken to what you are in He Who created you.

Do this simply by exchanging your own judgment for His perfect Judgment of you. His Judgment is as real as it is lasting. Nor does it ever change about you. He has kept His Judgment safe while you have failed, and offers it now to replace all mistakes you have made about yourself or others.

You need only receive the Gift of His Judgment now. For His is of light and happiness and will never leave or fail. Choose then to listen to it now, and let illusions from the past and fears of the future drop easily and quickly away.

Hide not your own darkened judgments, but bring each quickly to the light within you. Healing is of the light within, just as sickness in all forms arises from the darkness of your own failed judgments. You are never right. But He is always correct.

By bringing all judgment to Him first you will leave deception behind and heal.

And by offering a mind clear of deception and judgment to others, each will easily join with your heart in joy of recognizing Him together. And eternal truth will join you both and keep you joined with Heaven.

ON

ADDICTION
AND OBSESSION

On the whole, the words addiction and obsession mean almost the same thing.

Obsession applies more to people, places and things, while addiction applies more to a substance that is taken internally. However, we will use the word "addiction" while speaking about both ideas, since the idea of addiction is the basis for both.

The experience of addiction stems from fixation and then abuse. When you fixate on something or someone your compassion becomes a self-destructive and self-centered passion, allowing you to believe that without the subject or object of your desire you are no longer completely whole.

Medicine and magic are often the tools of an addict to both mask and prolong their own sense of false dependency and unwholesomeness. Unfortunately, by your own false dependence on a person, place or thing, you automatically project your need for reminder that you are whole onto them.

Without the object of your desire you are then left with a sense of emptiness that seems that only another "fix" can supply. This can occur with a close relationship, a drug or medication, food or otherwise. Whatever the addiction, it is a sure indication that somehow you have deprived yourself of your own spiritual food.

A physical addiction is only a symptom of an underlying spiritual deprivation. Somehow you have thus taken the world you have made to replace the Heaven your Father created for you, believing that somehow sensual offerings can fulfill you. Yet this can never be so.

No matter how much money, sex, food or other things you attempt to secure yourself with, you will never know true peace and happiness until you learn to look only to within you for answers. I have said before that you do not need to lose the world you live in, but you do need to give up your investment in it.

Obsession is a form of subtle addiction. When you fixate on people, places and things being placed in the order you would have them be, you forget your own emotional responsibility to yourself.

This is merely because you wish to avoid truly forgiving yourself for something that occurred in your past.

It is necessary at the point of recognition that you may be doing this, to stop the obsessing with the outside long enough to carefully look at what is really going on within your own thinking.

Trying to correct things on the outside is never as effective as allowing your mind to be changed about the actual importance of the outside.

Truly, there is nothing outside of you to change. And, even if you could change the outside, how could this really help you achieve inner peace? For as long as your own ego seeks to fix things outside you, it will always find something else to realign its fixation to when the task before is completed.

You can easily change feelings of compulsion, addiction and obsession into ones of serene letting go through a spiritual practice.

It is merely a matter of what you choose to value more. If you value only peace you will find only peace. If you value and are committed to chaos, then this is what you shall experience and retain.

Remember always that fixation and obsession are merely projections of your own chaotic ideas of scarcity and lack. You have everything and you lack nothing.

There is no need to change what is created whole. And since God is whole and He created you whole, you need do nothing to prove it otherwise. Remember this and you will remain free of addiction and obsession. Be at peace because you indeed are peace.

ON
RELATIONSHIP
AND MARRIAGE

Relationships are foundational to your life, to God and to this material you are being offered.

Without relationships you could not experience your Self and God. You have come here seemingly separate from both God and your brothers and sisters, but you have also come here to remember together that you are indeed not.

Marriage is a celebration to remind you that you are indeed not separate. In this celebration you receive reminders from God that demonstrate unequivocally that your oneness is fully established in Him.

A marriage celebrated with Him reaches out to everyone in celebration, and touches those whom you may never come into contact physically.

Marriage is already of God. Yet a marriage performed by man is a call for His remembrance for everyone. Holy matrimony under His Guidance reminds everyone that each is joined in His spiritual Oneness. Thus, the celebration of real marriage is one of the deepest reflections of your own holiness.

In the highest sense each of you are all already married in spirit. In Christ you are all as One. You need only recognize your Oneness by simply recognizing it in everyone you meet without exception. You find this difficult only because of your tendencies to earmark everyone you meet with certain personality traits, making each into separate "identities."

These identities, though real in your eyes, are but marks of false distinction made only by you. This is why you should learn not to judge another. All of your own judgment is of your own making and not of God's. He makes no distinction throughout His Kingdom. Nor need you make distinctions lest you believe you can usurp God's power for your own. You cannot. But together, you can share and enjoy the power of Love He has given you both to share equally.

Remember always that the special relationship is one you have established for your own conditions and expectations. Yet can these conditions be anything but your own limiting and imprisoning ideas? And by removing your own expectations and conditions can you not then expect to know the other as they truly are?

A holy relationship is one in which you have allowed God to establish His one healing condition for you. Can any relationship but this one be real?

Everyone who comes here makes special relationships. And each special relationship you make is brought to you for a higher reason that you may or may not recognize. Its higher purpose is to allow you to realize where you have placed special conditions on yourself, and then, heal them by letting them go.

Each condition you truly let go of brings you that much closer to recognizing Heaven. Each condition you withhold from Him brings you further into your own self-made hell. For you cannot hold conditions without believing in something other than Heaven.

Recognize, then, that marriage and relationships are not of your own making, but of He who created you through His own Heavenly Will. Thus the only way to fix a relationship is through God and His Love.

You cannot fix a relationship by analyzing it or breaking it down somehow. By doing so you are each participating in a process that is not healing you and is unworthy of you. For by analyzing the relationship you are merely working with the ego and its poor habits.

The ego is habitually poor and you will not change this. Instead, learn to overlook its fear, anger and hatred, choosing truth over deception, joining over the illusion of separation.

You who are already joined in heart and soul need only be reminded that it is so. Take then the hand of both those you call friend or enemy and recognize them both as the same. Do not shrink from the great responsibility God has given you to do so. You need no ceremony but the one Love has already easily provided you.

Celebrate with everyone you see and even those you don't and remember that God is with each of you together, holding you both in His gentle and loving arms. In Him and His Judgment there can be no separation or lines to separate you somehow.

His Gift is both your Oneness with Him and your sisters and brothers. Together, celebrate this Oneness without distinction of any kind. Place no name on another that is different from your own, and you will once again know what is yours together in Heaven.

ON
SEXUALITY

As the world sees it but not as God knows it, sexuality and guilt seem to go hand in hand.

This is merely because the ego associates the body with sexuality, which in turn entices the mind to believe that it is part of the bodily experience. It is actually quite the opposite. The body is always only secondary to the mind's experience, being the only place where real experience is possible.

The body can have no real experience of itself. But it is quite apparent that the ego does not believe this, otherwise you could and would not experience any guilt in association with it.

The fact that you do is an indication that you have falsely associated yourself as being only a body. The ego truly believes this, but the Holy Spirit knows this can never be so.

You should do your best in all cases never to associate yourself as a body. The body is merely a tool, and one in which can be used for lower or higher concerns, but never both at once. When you see your sexuality as merely a physical thing you disassociate yourself from spirit. The proper name for this biblically is lust.

It becomes seemingly sinful to you because you have temporarily lost touch with the spirit of your own creation and replaced it with lower thoughts about the body. This cannot harm what you truly are, but it can harm your ability to be aware of what you really are.

By seeing yourself as merely a body you automatically become overly dependent on the five senses for your own equation of what a real and lasting experience is.

By depending on the physical only, you slowly forget your own eternal spirituality. This invites numerous off-centered scenarios into your experience and distorts your own precious awareness of spirit as your true Self as God created you.

It makes you overly dependent on other bodies for your sense of inner peace, making it impossible to experience the total freedom that God created for your whole spiritual experience.

Sexual addiction can become as real for you as any other addiction because it makes the body your only priority.

It is very possible for you to experience your sexuality without experiencing the sense of lust, bodily glorification and addiction that often arises with it.

A committed relationship to only one partner will often help because eventually with your true commitment to only God's Love in each other you will each begin to break through one another's ego barriers, thus learning to focus on the true and spiritual aspects that are the same for both of you.

The depths of your own human sexuality are ingrained within the ego-made thought system. They one day shall pass. The depth of your own spirituality is created for you by God and merely need be accepted as His eternal Thought of you. This will never pass. Be so comforted by this understanding.

ON
FAMILY

In the truest sense, the idea of family belongs to spirit because spirit is united with everyone.

The family of God contains everything living and everything that seems no more. A family that forgets God has forgotten their own human family because every real family is created through God.

You should treat everyone you meet as family, for by forgetting no one as a part of you, you will remember what you are together. What you share will always be yours, as what you withhold will quickly seem lost to you.

The meaning of family is two or more of one kind sharing fully and equally the same Father who created them. In doing this, it sets up a foundation to be taken to every other living being.

You should look to everyone not for differences, but what is consistent and true for you both. If you look for only this, you will find your Origin together. This also requires a setting aside of ego goals by replacing them with only willingness and eagerness to heal together.

To heal is to find a common thread that fails not to ever unbind your recognition of being joined only in God's Family.

Within every human family there exists unloving behaviors as well as their underlying attitudes. These can more easily be understood as lacks of love, or, lapses in remembering to love.

The human family is about healing and recovering your ability to share God. Once recognized to be only in God's Family through this willingness to heal your humanness, you will be lifted in vision to see your greater family. You do not need another's presence to fully heal. Only your willingness is required.

Remember I have said that the ego's very function here is to get and not share. Getting while not giving requires manipulation often learned in childhood through certain implanted ideas of deprivation whether in this life or in a past one.

A simple formula for healing this is to demonstrate as much as possible only the awareness of love's abundance. It does take some effort to communicate love in your transactions, simply because true loving involves risk to your guarded and wanting ego.

Yet the benefits of fully giving for the needed healing of your hearts are indeed miraculous. It is what the world is lacking. But remember, abundance does not come from the world, but from within.

It is as simple as being still, listening to His loving Will, and acting on behalf of the loving spirit you have joined. Now, simply ask your sister and brother to join this pure spirit with you. You will know when this is accomplished, because joyous laughter will always follow for those who suddenly recognize they are one merely pretending to be two.

Since in most cases a family is close to each other in both getting and giving, the family is the one place where the greatest healing is possible. When you have learned to truly give of your Self to your own family you will remember that you are blessed in the whole human family as well. When you truly bless your own family you will then take your blessing to everyone.

In some cases, this action will or must be reversed, where you bless your friends and others in the world, and then your family. It is up to you what is most comfortable, but the results are equal and the same: recognition of your one enlightened Self and not the insane many that the ego tries to place between you and true vision.

You who want to serve, serve your own family first, and as you do your family will extend the service of Love to all. But let it begin with you.

For healing is always for you even though it extends itself outward to include everyone. When you accept the healing power of Love in your own life, situations will attract opportunities for you to share this light with all those you meet.

But do not mistake your self as the healer. Christ, who is everyone's Self, is the only true healer. It is also the only true you. Look for this grandeur everywhere in everyone, because there it is: beyond the senses and body's vision and only in the heart of everyone!

There are those in your family you or they may still hold a grudge towards, either him or her towards you, or you towards them. If so, you see them in your mind's eye right now. Do not let another moment go by without allowing the healing Rays of God's forgiving Light to shine upon each of them.

Forgive yourself for the picture of darkness that may still stick in your mind with anger. You know who they are. And they wait patiently for your blessing of Christ's total forgiveness upon them. Seek not their past, but look beyond what is gone forever and see in them now their lonely hearts calling you. They seek what you seek.

Their goal is one with your own. They want only what you both can share. And the light of God calls on you both to lay all hatred and anger down, and to accept the Gift that He has kept safe for you.

Offer His Gift of gentle forgiving light to the other with completely open arms, and share His Light willingly and openly. Do not be afraid to set your anger aside. But let God take your hatred from you now so that you may join with everyone in sweetest celebration that Christ in His Oneness has come, filling you each with the joy of remembering your oneness and your peace. For He has come! And His healing calls to everyone through you. Join Him now in His perfect and joyous calling. And let His perfect Answer be offered for everyone now.

ON
RECREATION, PLAY AND COMPETITION

Gentle playfulness can bring those who participate closer to each other and God.

The ego, however, looks at playfulness as a form of competition. When there are wages to be won and greatness to be gained, egocentricity often comes into to play, and the spirit of true playfulness is lost to that which is now feared to be "lost" or "gained."

As soon as the ego sees something to be gotten it automatically associates winning as everything. However, playing to simply play the game without thought of loss or gain can truly be an inspiring experience for those who are able to do so. By doing so, the emphasis is placed on having a joyous experience rather than a victorious one.

It should be understood that competitiveness is a civilized form of war. But it is still war, and the stakes spiritually are often the same for the untrained mind.

Those who participate in constant competition will often feel as though they are somehow being drugged. Constant competition on the high can lead to temporary exaltation, and on the low can lead to a deep sense of depression and loss of purpose when the competing is over. This is all because the process of constant competing is synthetic, and is like taking a drug.

In your true natural state you do not need to compete. Nor do you need to drug yourself. Both are states of mind invented by the ego merely to keep you preoccupied and out of reach from your true purpose, which is merely to forgive, be truly helpful and rejoice in the stillness of peace and Love.

So many of you go to work each day to compete and then come home only to share your competitiveness with your family, often projected as misdirected anger, and even hatred, which indeed is closer to describing the real problem. You see, you cannot be competitive without projecting some form of anger or hatred onto others and the world.

Since you made the world but do not yet believe it, you must indeed hate it because you believe in some way that it is unattainable. And so it is that you believe you must strike out to "beat the odds." This reinforces the idea that competition is your only method for survival.

Yet any mother would tell you that it is insane that a child would have to compete for her love. The child already has it though he may not believe it or realize it. Such is God's love for you. Your anger and competitiveness will not bring it closer to your awareness, but will actually take it further away.

Can you perhaps imagine a place where competition has been laid aside? A place where getting was entirely replaced by giving? It is never too late to let the idea of competitiveness be replaced by a true willingness to share the same Goal, which is certainly without darkened actions or conditions.

Genuine sharing is offering to live with others without your own future expectations or conditions, and to see them as they are only now: individual gifts from God to you. With nothing to take from them, you will know them and experience them as they truly are. Can any gift be greater than this?

The only form of competition that belongs in your mind is a form that is fully settled, forgiven, and thus, completely overcome. So in truth, you recognize its futility before it begins, and therefore, it never does begin. What began as playful has often before set great wars in motion.

Competition should thus be waged with a careful heart and mind. When a form of competition becomes personal, that person has lost his or her peace. Yet when competition is entirely inclusive and is ruled without winner and loser, and instead is shared and experienced equally no matter the seeming outcome, then and only then can joining together into a loving arrangement be fully experienced. And genuine playfulness abides here.

ON
CHILDREN
AND
PARENTING

There is only one real parent and one real child and both have one real name: the spirit of love.

You ask how you might discipline your children and still attend them with love? It is far better to ask how you might successfully discipline your own mind to still remain self-loving.

You cannot correctly assess, let alone discipline your own mental or emotional state while you alone put yourself in charge of any type of judgment and decision. If you did so you could expect the reaction of an angry child because in every direction you are misusing the idea of authority.

Remember, authority is not of you. Instead, it acts through you without judgment. This is precisely why only God's Authority works. Contemplate this. Always ask first for the Holy Spirit's happy Decision. You will know it is God's judgment by its lack of negative or painful charge. And others will react peacefully to it because the Authority is indeed peaceful, as well as being derived from above you and not of you.

Remember that children naturally uncover unhealed and childish reactions from parents and adults. Children will seek true spiritual discipline as well as truly loving attention. If they try and get it by purposely working to make you angry, there may be a good chance they are merely reflecting a form of your own non-presence towards them.

A cycle of negative attention getting is most often easily broken at whatever point you decide to become truly present, loving and communicative as a parent towards them. Children need child-like attention as well from parents. In other words, it is equally as important for a parent to honestly, lovingly and gently embrace their children.

A healing family is guided by spirit to let go of the need to intellectualize, as well as rationalizing. You cannot join hearts with your own child as long as you persist in maintaining a mere disciplinary role. And a child cannot mature emotionally unless he or she learns to make decisions based on more than mere rational thinking. So many parents fear letting go of the disciplinary role as "the parent," and they forget that their children will someday be parents as well.

You would do well to remember that everyone has a child, parent and adult built into their own psyche, and thus, their own way of learned acting on each of their behalves. An imbalance can cause a parent to act more like a child while the child is acting more like the parent. Ask the Holy Spirit to correct this by deciding for you for your children.

Everyone at some point plays the role of both a child and a parent. And everyone at some point is a child or parent. Everyone. But no matter how old you believe you are, you are always a child in God's Mind. This is the real, the humble, and the forgiven you.

Where parenting is concerned, a child begins to learn the art of parenting at a very young age. Acting as a child or a parent is just that—acting. If you remove the roles and the acting you will always come closer to the gentle Self God created as you.

And thus, you will naturally become closer to the others in your life. You are not here to be an actor, but instead to grow into a healing teacher and a real learner, that is, a genuine loving presence to all with all of you.

The balance of these two ideals will overcome the previous tendency towards being seen as an "actor parent" or an "actor child." This sounds highly descriptive and complex, yet in practice it is indeed quite simple and natural. A truly loving act is many times wordless. Remember this, Holy child.

When you have finally overcome the need to act a role as either parent or child you will come into the true awareness and remembrance of your eternal and One Self, that is, the Self God created as you. In this sense you are an adult-child of God. Yet the simplicity of this can be described as light connecting with Itself.

Parenting a child to rely on the Self you share with them is an understood and demonstrated procedure, not a taught one. This is where many good intentioned parents have lost their intimate connection with family, because they were taught one thing and shown another. What is learned is taught, but what is demonstrated of love is constantly re-remembered, celebrated and lived. Quite a difference!

As a parent it is up to you to do your best to demonstrate only love to your children. To do so is to help them and yourselves to overcome the world and remember you are truly one with God. How important is the family role!

ON
DISEASE, SICKNESS AND MEDICATION

Every disease and sickness you encounter is self-made and you can change your mind about it.

In healing from it do not make the mistake of trying to separate from it, for sickness is made in the mind where it is also healed. Instead, invite the illness from your mind and body into your own heart where it can be healed.

Do not fear it, for fear was made to overcome love, which it can never really do. Do not be angered by it, which will only tend to increase its hold on the body. Instead, give the illness a name, and then, let the light of God's love shine upon it, and then through it, washing away its feared darkness and suffering. Place your eternal Self in charge of both healing it and washing it away.

A sickness can be feared enough to get a hold on you that is both gripping and painful. Yet you must ask yourself, "What am I holding onto?" Ask yourself honestly if you are clinging more to the pain than you are to life?

The actual fear and avoidance of disease is often exactly what is originally behind making it in the first place.

Avoidance is always behind any increase in fear. Rather than avoid, risk inviting the sense of physical disease into your emotional center where the disease was made and where it will heal.

The body will heal as the mind heals the conditions it was holding onto. These conditions may be towards yourself or another, but in the end they always affect you first.

In sickness you are made to suffer, a plan that is widely recognized by the ego, which it stands thoroughly behind in every way. Sickness is its "proof" that you are weak and without an awareness of spirit. Sickness is "proof" that you are merely a flawed body, destined for death and then hell.

Yet there is one thing the false idea of sickness cannot prevail upon: the fact that you are spirit and deciding to recognize this leads to its complete undoing.

Where spirit is remembered, sickness is emotionally left behind. And a decision for healing is essential for any true healing to occur, remembering, of course, that healing is emotional.

Not everyone will choose to heal a disease they have succumbed to. Not everyone can. Often times the particular disease is specifically chosen as a timely form of the denial of love. Everyone denies the love that would save at some time. This is part of your choice to embrace humanity.

Yet it is essential to eventually remember the great Force in you that is behind all healing whether your body is ill now or not.

When you remember your Source you will truly not fear anything again, acknowledging that the fear of death is often a factor in increasing a sicknesses hold on you.

Do not look to the body for healing to occur. The body is nothing by itself, and only demonstrates the beliefs you have placed upon it. Believe instead in the power of your one Mind, which in itself can never die.

Your mind is created for you, which you cannot alter. Yet you can indeed change the focus of where your mind is centered by changing your mind about what your mind has implanted within its beliefs.

It is hard for the sick to believe that medication is merely a form of magic, just as a disease is. Yet this is all it is, and is a temporary solution at best. The mind is the only permanent solution for a physical state that is at best temporary. Change your mind about the body, and do what is entirely lovable and loving for your mind so that the body shall perhaps follow.

A right mind is a clear and exercised mind, and free of the past and future as well. Would you not agree that this is eventually the one mark you must choose? The body cannot exercise the mind, but the mind can choose to exercise the body, and must do so in the holy present for both to work in close harmony.

Indeed, the word "healthy" and the word "healing" imply degrees, opposites and comparisons. Better, however, to perceive a loving solution instead of "healthy degrees". Degrees imply a measurement, while a loving solution confirms one firm and happy decision. A loving solution can therefore not be partial because it confirms your own creation in God.

ON
HEALING, HEALTH AND MEDICINE

In truth, healing is all you truly came here to do.

Everyone heals whether they realize it or not. And those who do heal realize that they are not the true healer, but the healed. You heal as you become willing to heal with others. And all healing is through God.

The recognition that you are not a body is the prerequisite for true healing. Those who are endowed with the recognition of God's love must begin to heal because true healing is never of this world, but of the One who created you. His healing is called upon through the activation of the Holy Spirit, whose quiet and gentle hand washes away all pain and fear.

If you do not hear the Holy Spirit it is because you have allowed fear to distract you. Do not punish yourself because at times you cannot hear. Everyone, no matter how devoted, becomes distracted from love at some time. Instead, learn to flow with the river of spirit inside you. Pay not to the attention of what is on the shore. Instead, listen within, past all the mumblings of anger and fear, and find the still waters within that would heal.

Your inner peace is your inner health. Find your center in God and do not waver from its light! Listen to the gentle Voice of the Holy Spirit as He heals all suffering and pain. He is with you always, no matter how it may seem. Simply become quiet and listen ever so carefully to the quiet sound of His Love. He has not abandoned you. But in your fear and anguish you have abandoned Him.

Choose now to receive His spirit back into your heart. Your heart has much room for He who always loves you. Yet you cannot know this until you are willing to place resentment and anger aside, even if only for a few moments. Listen willingly and in quiet gentleness He will come.

There is no medicine greater in strength than God's. He will help you to where your medicine can never take you. Do not be afraid, however, to rely on forms of the world's medicine when you feel you need to. You are not expected to remember your sainthood while sickened and weak. Use what is at your disposal to help the body restore its strength, while also turning inward to God for spiritual strength.

Healing is the natural profession of all God's children. Yet so few understand the power of love because they have exchanged it for the medicine of the world, be it money, power or drugs. Do not further exchange your own great Power for what can only give you temporary help and satisfaction.

You cannot feel the power of God's Healing Rays until you are willing to share this love with everyone. Yet let go of the conditions you have placed on others and you will instantly begin to truly heal. Do not set your conditions aside begrudgingly, but instead with great elation! For this is the first step in the beginning of your own true and lasting healing!

It has been asked many times in many different ways why so many are plagued by their own self-hatred. Self-hatred, of course, is conditioned into your experience by the development of your belief in time, and thus, your followed disbelief in the eternal. With this belief came guilt, that is, the idea that each of your mistakes, big or little, may indeed follow you all through time and even into eternity when you die.

The ego does not discern when it comes to punishment, for it believes that even unto death a part of you will still "live" to be punished. This is exactly why the ego has been so difficult for a majority of you to transcend.

Yet let me be clear here: every mistake you think you have ever made has been one that is somehow dependent on the physical. I have repeatedly said that the physical is not a part of God or your own Reality. Why then would you believe that any of your mistakes in time really matter?

These mistakes are simply decisions not to love, small or large periods of time you have measured and judged as unworthy of praise or love, and you believe sickness is a form of punishment from He who created you.

Yet why would God punish any one of you when He has not even seen your mistakes in time? They matter not to Him because His World, as is yours, is only Heaven! And this He will readily realize for you anytime you are truly willing to set your forms of hatred quickly down.

The Holy Spirit is the only one who can discern between the loving and the fearful. If a thought is fearful, He merely overlooks it by not recognizing it at all. By following His loving judgment you are immediately taken to a Place that is transcendent of all judgment.

This Place is devoid of fear because it speaks a language not understood by the world. In Heaven only that which leads to It can enter with you. The sounds and sight of Heaven transcend physical sound and sight. Sound and sight are given entirely new meaning within It's Gates. No hatred will ever enter the Kingdom you are one with. No punishment shall ever be shown before God.

You must be entirely and honestly willing to ask your Self, (Christ),"Why do I insist on hating myself and punishing myself?" You must learn to remember that when you are hatefully critical of yourself or anyone you are allowing your mind and heart to slip away from God's Hands and back into your own alone.

If you ask truly, the Holy Spirit will gently remind you that God could never hurt you, and that trying to hurt yourself in any form is always reflected in your relationships with your brothers and sisters. For when attack occurs in any form towards another, you are giving your precious time over to a dictator that will happily use the attack to further imprison your will and make you feel ever so small.

Do not make this mistake my loving sisters and brothers! You have not the time to be disorderly for any longer! Do not give credence to any form of hatred, for you will never be truly comfortable with even the smallest part of hatred and anger in your hearts and minds again!

I have come again to show you your value, and to show you that your grandeur has always been with you and in you. You are not small! You are not unworthy! You are not hateful or discouraged. You have been given every capacity for healing that is in God's Mind! Use it while you have time and do not look away from the joyous and uniting results of what it will always offer you now!

There will always be medicines for you to depend on so long as the world remains. Up until now our focus has been more on healing in this section. I have not come to tell you to abandon your reliance on different forms of medication. Most of the medications you each take are needed because you have temporarily been unable to allow your loving Spirit within to heal your own frightened mind.

You are not expected to be rendered into an awareness of your own perfect state just because I am telling you it is indeed so. You are merely asked to take small steps to ask for Help more increasingly so that true emotional healing can begin.

Do not wonder why God has not healed your physical ills. If He were to do so without your truly asking and genuine preparedness, you would likely become even more fearful than before, thus making the illness have an even greater hold on you.

Focus on bodily healing is a misstep because all healing is in the mind where sickness originated. Look, then, for spiritual light within first. Enlightenment and peace are not dependent on bodily woes. Remember this always.

First, realize that if you are ill you have somehow asked for its form to help you return to Love. Do not forget this little child. And do not forget that your true escape from numbness depends on your own emotional focus, and thus, harmonizing, enlightening decisions. The dark emotions you are repressing are what make you physically ill. No, not usually. Always!

The human ego is like an iceberg. Beneath your worldly conscious state of mind is a machine of suppression that you once made to replace God. You brought these separation thoughts with you even before you were "born."

The mind now believes that the key to its survival is this dark machine made of an illusory history and time. You are taught in the world of time to keep your machine "well oiled," through education, technology and science. This is merely the ego's way of insuring what it sees as its own guaranteed survival.

Survival of the body is what is needed for the ego to believe that its own experience in the world is indeed real. It cannot be said enough and in more than enough ways: the ego, the body and its entire experience here is already null and void, for everything experienced from a merely physical standpoint has been and will always be a mere fantasy.

It is your idea of some form of replacement for love. It cannot and will never last, for it is not love, but a shabby deception to keep you from the real experience of Love God has always kept for you.

You cannot experience this Love until you become entirely willing to heal as God would heal you. You cannot begin to truly heal until you completely give up making up your own reality from a mere dream.

I have said this before. But now I must emphasize this in deep hope that you will hear my call for you to return your mind and heart back to Heaven with me. I cannot release you from the nightmare until you become fully willing and fully ready for another Reality.

Eternal Reality is forever yours and offers you everlasting Safety. There is nothing that can substitute for It because no substitute for Love has really ever lived. Yet you are Life as God created you. But this Life cannot be embraced until you let go entirely and fall away from your earthly restraints and addictions.

I have said to have all give all to all. Do not underestimate this statement, as it can only promise your full release from all hatred, anger and suffering.

Let go, my child, of all the world's aspirations! There are none worthy of what you indeed are. Let fully go and become once again fully willing and fully giving, fully functional and fully loving. This is what you are created for: to forgive the world and gently return to awareness of eternal Love with all, and, secondly, to rejoice in this perfectly harmonious awareness.

The purpose of creation is to share the recognition of God's oneness as Itself. It is everywhere should you become fully and truly humble and willing. For you are

God's sons and daughters. Your function is to forgive; your purpose is love and loving. Your real and quiet mind is in the Heart of God.

ON
CATASTROPHE
AND
ACCIDENTS

For some of those who feed their anger from receiving "bad news," it may be difficult to accept that everything that seems to happen in your world happens without accident, yet it does.

It does not follow, however, that it should matter.

An accident, as you see it, is merely your perceptive interpretation of a situation in which one or more people were not entirely awake or conscious, and therefore not fully aware of a present situation they might have found themselves in.

Accidents happen when one or two people are not being fully aware. Catastrophes occur when many people are choosing not to be fully aware of what they are choosing and what is really going on around them.

Full and complete awareness of your present situation is difficult to achieve for most of you. But you can learn to attune your minds only to what is happening now. By doing so you make yourselves less susceptible to what you may now term "an accident," and learn to interpret accidents more as a form of simple ignorance.

By becoming aware of God in everyone you see and meet, you reduce the events of catastrophe and accidents. Awareness is only genuine in this instant. That which you are aware of that is not in this instant is illusion or misperception.

You may find that most of your life is being lived in the illusory through the above measurement. Let this then help you to become aware of how often you dream instead of living free in the presence of your real life!

The consequence of living in a dream world is apparent on your news channel every day, and by the laws you have made to confuse and send you adrift of the love that is real.

All of you want so much to live happily and free in the present, but are usually too busy making future plans. One reason for this is that most of you are afraid to really love yourself and others in the moment. You fear that genuine love would take from you all your plans and fantasies, and this is indeed true. But you would not be unhappy because of this. In truth, you would be free and all the more lovable!

The greatest catastrophe is the fact that most of you still believe that you are indeed separate from God. Indeed, your own thinking is separate from both the truth and God.

But thinking is not a fact. You are inclined to believe that your thinking is indeed a fact, and this one mistake is what keeps you from experiencing Heaven with every-one you meet.

Try instead to become aware in each new moment that what you are thinking is never a fact, but merely your own private fantasy, not to be taken seriously, but laughed about because it is merely a fantasy and that is all. The less you take your own thinking seriously, the less you will take others as well. When you can laugh at perception because it is only a perception, you will be healed.

The extreme attraction you each have is that of being drawn to problems instead of answers. Your existence seems dependent on this. Without your reliance on the world's woes you often feel empty inside, as if there is nothing that would remind you that you are indeed alive except for the tragedy seeming to occur all around you.

What if I were to tell you that these forms of darkness and fear are all but meaningless tricks to keep you from your real purpose of forgiving, truly helping and experiencing a real sense of one's lovingness?

If you knew that you truly only had a few more moments to go before you could ever see your brother and sister again, would you stop running amuck and simply hold them? Would you stop acting so busy and insane and simply let go and love them now?

This is exactly what you each need to do now. There is so little time, for so much has been wasted making other plans. Will your other plans help you to remember Heaven? No. You will not need any one of them. And you will be glad those plans have not followed you. In fact, you will be delighted! And you will sigh in relief that you are finally safe and unafraid!

God will shine unto you completeness and you will then have only need of Him. He has kept everything and everyone you have and ever will cherish. Many of them wait for you glad return to greet them.

The catastrophes of the world are never met in Heaven. Nor need you leave the world to remember your place in His Kingdom. Merely stop looking for your answers where they cannot be. Come, join with me, and with all, and return Home to He who has always loved you, and kept for you His grand creation! His creation is joy. Share only of this and be returned to the awareness that you are pure, and whole, and wholly loving and forever lovable!

ON
HATRED
AND
DAMNATION

The world is but a projection of your belief in separation, and thus, hatred.

Each of you thinks you have found the right religion, the right way, the right formula to return you someday to Heaven. And since you are so sure that your way is the right way, you have come now to defend this system you have so long ago adopted. You have learned that to secure the future you must defend and uphold the ways from the past that seemed to have once worked.

Yet you do not realize the danger this has put you in. For time and history are fully dependent on ignoring God. The past made real in the present is how the ego would hope to maintain this delusion. And yet how long can the illusion of darkness really last? No time at all! It was gone the moment it seemed possible that darkness had arisen.

Hatred is the dream, and damnation is the dream destroying itself. There is nothing to love about the world because it is a picture of the illusion of struggle and darkness. It represents the "devil's" effort to make the separation from Love real. And indeed, you do believe this struggle is real, and even that the devil (ego) is winning the war! Little child, this is simply not so.

You do not realize that since time began, the ego has repeatedly made the exact same mistake over and over again. And while time is still measured as your form of reality, it will seem to go on. Time is not what is really important in this sorrowful world made by fear. Healing is. Healing is what will undo the need for time, and thus, time itself will disappear.

The undoing of the world will be accomplished by You, through God. You who are many and are so tired of the world rejoice! The Great Alternative is here. You need not fear what you have so long asked for. The carpet of time is rolling up and God's gentle sleeve is rolling down. His Rapture will be the end of suffering, the end of time, and the end of all fear and hatred. And those who seem to need Him not now will need Him soon. Yet soon is now. Be mistaken not. The time of the eternal One is at hand and so soon will time be no more.

Yet you who remain awhile as miracle workers must send His clear message: His Safety is in you and nowhere else. No longer look outside for any form of comfort, for it will surely fail you as it always has. Yet the stress of this vacillation between the world and God is surely becoming acute.

Nowhere in the world is a haven of temporary happiness left. Nowhere can anyone hide from His Light. For those who try will suffer only more. For those who hold on to worldly possessions out of fear will begin to crumble into humility.

There is no escape left for ones who would somehow excuse themselves from the rest. You are all together or you are not at all. God knows His Son is one, and so there will be no more holding out. The selfishness will be shed as if a skin off a snake in the hot desert. And my child, your weight will be all the less from the giving up.

Hold on no longer to what was never yours! You were not created mad. Nor were you created to hate. You are but mere children who do not know the repercussions of their own mistaken actions. You are not damned for your greed and withholding. You have simply become numb to God's Will on earth. It is no different here than in Heaven, my child.

The only way any one of you is damned is if the ego is real and God is dead. There may be some who really believe that this has occurred. Or, that it is occurring now. What is really occurring is that the child's sharp toys are being gently taken from him. For they cannot help you achieve the state of mind that Heaven has in store for you!

Let go and rediscover your eternal innocence child of Heaven! For it is all you have left. In fact, it is all you ever really had. Be as gentle with others as you know God will be with you. Help one another to shed the skin of apathy, self-loathing and self-centeredness.

Go with me to a Place where there is no time, and, no hurry to achieve what can never be achieved. Your hatred is already gone! For it is already healed. For it has fallen away with your ego long, long ago. And what you imagine has followed you in darkness has never really been. Not one shred of hatred remains. Not one shred of possibility for damnation of your self or your sister or brother exists.

You will forever have to live with your Self, for the end of the world can never take what God created from you. But do you know your Self? Do you really know your own created, eternal innocence?

Rejoice, rejoice, rejoice! I am come into the world as an eternal light with you to demonstrate that no guilt and no hatred are appropriate on earth or in Heaven. For Heaven is clean of all darkness as so shall the earth become.

Leave the skin of death completely behind and be reborn in pure joy and love now. This is the Place you were conceived of. This is the Place you have never really left. For now you can remember that your dreams of darkness and separation have been but dreams and that is all!

Awaken and shine with His Presence shining throughout you. Let His Light and only this Light flow through you as you are truly lifted into Heaven's Rapture. For you are not of the flesh, but of the Holy Light that created eternal Creation. You are Home only here, for it is this longing you are now beginning to remember. Allow its Presence, child. Allow its Presence and be enveloped by Heaven. Share only this with all without exception, for the reward is very soon to be the mightiest and greatest of all!

ON
ABORTION
AND
STILLBIRTH

In all things child, step back and let Him now lead the way.

The Holy Spirit is with you always and so you need never fear. You need not do and you need not change the world. No death can come to you who are part of Him. I bring you now a compassionate message to mothers and mothers to be.

You who have once lost a child giving birth or through other means must recognize this: you have lost no one because God has lost no one. You may give birth to many children, but never allow yourself to believe that you have somehow created them. The children are not yours. They are God's.

When a child is lost to you early in life by an accident, stillbirth or an illness, the great tendency for every mother is to blame herself. Yet you must realize that you no more created them than you created yourself. And merely because a human form is gone does not mean that the being is really gone. Gone from this world, yes. But gone altogether—of course not!

There is nothing that can take your children from your heart. And you should remember this because you are often apt to try to forget after a time when tragedy seems to have struck. This is a particularly harsh form of self-punishment that you should not incur.

The Holy Spirit, in fact, asks you not to forget the essence and being of this child. Nor should you ever be anything but grateful for the gifts they brought to you. They are ongoing! Some of the gifts a child brings come in the form of negative attitudes and behaviors as well. These negatives are often more important than the positive ones, simply because of how you once reacted to them.

Now that the child is gone you may be left with a sense of anger, emptiness and even hatred at both the child and God. Do not allow yourself to feel guilty because of this, and do not turn away from the darkness it may have seemed to have left you in. The anger and the darkness were not the child's gift to you. You had these darkened emotions already.

The child's gift to you was the fact that she or he opened your heart and mind to what you once kept well hidden in you. The pain you have always held, but away from conscious view. Now, because of the child's gift, the iceberg has begun to surface and melt, and it is not a nice feeling. Who is to blame? No one! Who is to thank? The child.

Be grateful, then, for the gifts the child has brought to you. And remember: every gift a child brings is not always in a loving form, for they, too, are your teachers. And as teachers they will find in you what you do not always wish to see. Precisely, this is part of the function of all of God's teachers.

Children are natural teachers. So listen to them while they are here, so you will not hurt so much when they may disappear—into life or into death. And remember, death is merely a different state of mind. It has perhaps fewer bells and whistles, but it is a consistently abundant, safe and loving place to be! Best of all, Heaven is real.

And now about abortion, since you have asked. This is a subject that is most often a communication breaker for most of you.

If God is eternal and as His creation you are eternal as well, taking birth into the world must be a way to forget this fact. And for most you have forgotten. Otherwise your key interests would be on helping others instead of your own single survival.

Birth into the body hardly interests God who is only interested in your remembering Heaven. The body is a shield against this remembering because it preoccupies the mind with the mere task of helping the body survive.

If you are to overcome the body and the world and truly receive Christ you must be entirely willing to overlook your assessment of what others do with their bodies, as well as, in fact, your own.

This sounds difficult, but I assure you, it is simply a decision of whether you allow time to supersede the eternal in you. It is a slight of hand by the ego to tempt you to place your concerns where they indeed do not belong. I have said that everything you ever need is given you because joy increases by extending it.

How can you know joy when you are constantly concerned with other people's decisions about anything? You cannot judge a decision by another no matter how extreme it may seem because it does not belong to you. Your brothers and sisters decisions may overlap into a part of your own life, yet ultimately you decide by your own response to it. This freedom cannot be taken away because it is built into your creation.

Your laws are made to decide for other bodies. Your laws are not for the mind, ever, because they entail some form of punishment or restriction on the body. These are believed necessary to impose some sense of order.

Yet historically and in the long run, how well has this really worked for you? Your prisons are filled and your crimes grow and grow. More laws are made and still the increase in violation continues. Could it be that the system based on control is faulty? Try to control an angry child and see how he or she reacts? Case in point. Forgiveness and love without condition no matter what is all that will ever work. Growth occurs with God's Love no matter what.

Let the ego make its case for as long as it wants, for it will be shorter and not longer. God's Plan has not changed. To atone for your guilt and hatred you must come only to Him. He can release you and no one else. The ego can imprison you and nothing else. The ego is indeed nothing because of its useless acts and results. Please, little child, remember these words in your heart!

ON
THE ELDERLY

By all appearances, those who are considered old are often left by the wayside.

You often treat the elders as if they are problem children, leaving them to feel isolated or as if their life is a burden to others. Your reaction to the old ones is often similar to how you might react to a little child. Yet in becoming old they have an attribute that the young have very little acquaintance with. They are often much more in tune with what is really and truly important: eternal wisdom.

For they have often learned the little importance of the world. They may not take seriously what you would want them to take seriously. They may offer more silence in their conversation with you. And some dwell so much on the past they make some uncomfortable.

Your ego is often bent on somehow getting them out of the way. The ego cannot find attributes in the old ones that it deems useful. And so it will pretend to listen while it agrees and patronizes to hopefully get them out of the way quicker.

It is important that you recognize that what you believe is valuable is likely not worthy of any consideration at all. And what is truly valuable is likely to be overlooked because of your intense belief in time. You are apt to believe that time is being wasted when speaking to a strange child, or an elderly person. Your focus is so often intent on taking care of business that you miss what is truly valuable.

You patronize both children and the elderly by pacifying them with a false sense of patience and gentleness. You are not really interested in what they have to say, mainly because you see your own current agenda as much more important than any possibility of experiencing a real relationship, and which could instantly change your evaluation of what your own life is for.

Currently, most of you are much more focused on what you own or what you could own soon. This measures your success. And so when success in the world realized, you pride yourself in your own belief in the illusion of security that you have made.

The elderly have often discovered what the younger ones have not: that true success can never involve the world at all! You may believe that what I am saying is insane. This is merely because you have deluded yourself so successfully in to believing that your own dreams are real, that any threat to that dream becomes a hindrance which you believe should be avoided at whatever cost you can bargain for. Yet you bargain with only insanity. And a wise elder knows that your dream will never last.

Therefore, in the eyes of wisdom, your dreams may not be taken seriously. And so, what you may believe to be wasted is merely the ego's poor evaluation of every situation. By listening to the ego your focus merely becomes self-centered and ego preserving.

Let the wiser and older teach you to be patient and teachable. You have often forgotten how to be a good student as well as a good listener. The ego is so entirely bent on getting as opposed to sharing that those who have listened to it have shut their own hearts and cut their own minds off from the miracle. Let your mind be open to the miracle with everyone by opening within you to the Heart of your oneness and gentle compassion.

The miracle is merely an instant of true communication of the Oneness shared by you and your brother and sister. Do not judge for yourself which people are worthy of compassionate attention. The Holy Spirit discards no one from the miracle.

Adopt His inclusive system without reservation or judgment. It is not so difficult. It is merely your own decision to not judge or even think about it. Disown your own thinking and wake up and become joyous with everyone!

Eternity will spring into any heart and mind that does so. But you must be willing to fully engage this decision. And by doing so, you will remember and help all others to remember. Not by your words, but by the dependable state of mind that exudes true joy and happiness. True enlightenment is but the recognition of the One Mind in all.

ON
EUTHANASIA
AND
SUICIDE

The decision for euthanasia or suicide is, of course, not a sinful one.

For if your life were solely dependent on the body, then it would be. The reason that sin does not really exist is merely because God created you from Himself. How can the eternal be hurt except in darkened dreams? No dream can hurt any child of God. Yet he or she can think they are hurt, and so the hurt becomes real for them. Whatever belief you choose to believe, remember this always: you are not a body and so you must be safe.

It is not the desire of God for anyone to remain more connected to a physical state than a spiritual state. The body is not really alive. It remains neutral until the mind decides to use it otherwise. Then it is seen by others as a way to identify a positive or a negative person. Yet you are no more a person than I am! The person you see as yourself, or, the person you see as another is merely a decision of the ego to misidentify both, and thus, cause a sense of separation instead of unity.

Your eyes cannot see, your ears will never hear, though the Son of God, Christ Himself, is where you all abide. You fool yourself, little child! You are used to believing in the little and the small. You have come to easily accept them both as attributes of yourself. How mistaken are you who accept only this limited state as your own reality!

The world has laws against suicide, although few who have committed the crime have ended up in jail. And remember, Heaven is a place of joy and laughter! And so, how should you judge the act of taking ones own life? You need not judge it at all. Instead, accept happily the path this brother or sister has taken. You believe you must grieve for them. Why? They are not grieving!

The ego dresses you in black with a veil, telling you to look down to the ground where your body is buried. The ego's funeral is such a celebration of the bleak and black. Mourn this body's death forever and ever, for you will never see this one you loved again.

Please, please! There is no separation in Heaven! You are all together or you are all separate, as the ego would teach you. Yet what is the part of your own mind that sees itself as separate from another as well as separate from Heaven?

If living is a form of forgetting Heaven then what is this life you seem so attached to really? Is it not a form of death you have somehow in your own sick way become attached to? You yield nothing but pain and sorrow from it and then celebrate its end with more blackness!

The rituals of the ego are long and many, but none are more well dramatized then that of its great celebration of death. Mourn for your poor brother and sister who reminds you that you may be next to join the parade of darkness. And where has your remembrance of Life gone for you who have adapted this bleakness?

You cannot see eternity though it has never left you. You cannot see it because in the numbness you have accepted you cannot feel it. You have forgotten the moment of loving and exchanged it for a seemingly timeless hatred. Yet with this darkness in mind, how is it that your heart has always survived?

You are here now, being reached out to by Christ, who only holds your compassionate best interest in heart and mind. It is here for you right now! Will you not claim this invisible compassion, and offer its visibility to others by acting with me in the light of compassionate love?

It is never up to you to decide for another unless the other is so incapacitated that they cannot decide for themselves. When this occurs those who are deemed compassionate and who are without fear of life and death decisions should make the decision. This one or ones should be able to decide without passion and morality standing in the way.

God wills that none of His children should suffer. Since all suffering is based in misperception, a life or death decision should be made by those clear of mind and heart and without fear of judgment from man or God. Since only men judge in the wrong sense, God will open His Heart to those who decide in everything with compassion and without condition.

And, as always, remember to ask the Holy Spirit in every decision. Wait for His Answer, as He will never fail you. His Decision may not be the decision of the world. But, it is always the decision of Heaven. His gentle decision is always your answer to every problem. Often it will not make the whole world happy. But, it will indeed make you happy. And you are indeed important and worthy of joy and happiness.

Ask first always, and He will never let you down. You will know that you have shared in His Decision by the attitude it brings with it. For if the decision is bona fide, nothing but peace and serenity will forever follow.

Amen

ON
DEATH
AND DYING

By now, you who believe you are in the world must think you are experts on death and dying.

For this is the way of the world. You consider it murder if one kills another. Yet you start wars and then justify murder and pardon the ones your powers have given "permission" to do so. You call these deaths not murder, but "statistics."

How strange are your laws and rationalizations. Even yet, those who kill another without permission are subject to a death penalty: an eye for an eye without permission, and, as many as you can take out with permission.

In your world you have set certain rules for taking a life. And you have saved certain punishments for those rules that have been broken. Did God give certain men extraordinary powers for dealing with these rules? Did He have a part in their making?

If your answer is yes, you do not know God! For God's Law is only that He created you. And for this you are eternal. Therefore you may accept this one spiritual rule: You cannot be hurt or destroyed by any law or any act of man. To take the body away from one who has killed another is not experienced as punishment, but as freedom from every human downfall.

When the world has passed there will be no more hatred. There will be no more punishment. There will be no more guilt. For only in the world of bodies can such an immersing illusion seem to exist. Your very existence is defined by this illusion. For without your own self-devised pain and punishment how else would you know you are alive?

Human life has a funny rule. Those who cling to it must suffer. Those who truly do not fear dying seem to discover their own resurrection. Then how does one not fear her or his own death? It is most simple. You refrain from the judgment of others thus avoiding judgment for yourself! Could it be that simple? I have said it is so. And so, little child, believe and accept this simple truth, and then, practice it wholeheartedly!

To practice this effectively one must entirely forgive the past, thus freeing the future to remain only in the present. It is easily said but not always so easily done. Why? Each of you on an unconscious level carries around an iceberg of deep and well-hidden hatred, and thus, guilt. I have spoke on this before, but it is now time to acknowledge it together.

It is this dark hatred that you seek to heal in your very special and intimate relationships. I have said that so often a new intimate relationship begins with a feeling of discovering Heaven. And this is indeed true. Yet why is it that it never seems to last? What begins as non-egotistical more often than not turns into flaming hatred towards the other partner.

And as I have already said, when you find this special partner your deep down hope is for him or her to save you from your hatred. Yet the knight in shining armor slowly deteriorates into a prison guard who seems to hold the key to your own freedom and enlightenment.

Many have heard the phrase, "Die before death and live forever." This is so true. But ask yourself honestly, "What must die?" Is it you who dies or is it merely the ego state which you find yourself living mostly in? Without your own separatist thinking, what would be you?

To discover this there is risk involved because you are so attached to your own dreams that you think about them constantly, reinventing them over and over again, and suffering when they do not manifest as you would want them to.

For instance, the bank calls and says you are overdrawn. How do you deal this? Do you become angry and upset? Or are you able to recognize it as only a part of your own dream? Can you awaken when you are judging the dream, or when you are angry at something in the dream? Of course not, because you have made the dream your "reality" for the time being, or until you choose to see the situation differently.

How can you see it differently? By simply recognizing that it is only a dream. And this is done with your constant vigilance to living within the mental framework of true forgiveness. You recognize that the nightmare is but a dream and then choose to simply awaken.

And the Holy Spirit will always help you if you but ask Him. Ask Him as often as you forget that you are merely dreaming, and have Him re-remind you to simply awaken in the present moment and be free.

ON

AGREEMENTS, INTEGRITY AND COMMITMENT

Agreements and commitments made in the integrity of the ego never last in eternity.

Your good intentions do not exist in the light of eternal Love. An agreement made in Love contains the eternal Source of the Universe as its foundation. In truly loving agreements comes the recognition of perfect safety. These agreements are not bound in guilt or blame, but by eternal Love all alone, and become the enlightening and joining commitments that undo the need for time and the world. Commitments made in this loving sense are everlasting, merely because the Foundation is pure and with a purpose that goes far beyond the world.

The attempt to hold agreements and commitments with integrity is but your attempt at good intentions without the presence of the Holy Spirit. Your good intentions will never bring you the peace you truly desire. The peace and Oneness that you and your brothers and sisters truly desire as a child of God can only be attained through your awareness of your holiness, that is, your true nature given to you by God.

No amount of agreements or commitments can give you the joining, Oneness and freedom that your brothers and sisters truly are. If you have made an agreement that is binding you or that hurts you somehow, you need the help of the Holy Spirit to lead you back to the right path: the path that will benefit you and all who are included the most, and the most peacefully.

The key to healing one's life is the willingness to allow the healing of your mind. Everyone who is here is in a dream. I am attempting to lead you to awaken from this dream. In order for you to awaken, you must forgive the perception of a separated world. It is not enough to merely tell you that the hateful and darkened nightmares you sometimes live in are merely your own unforgiven illusions.

Yet why is it that it may seem to you that the same nightmare comes to haunt you again and again? The bad dreams that come again and again in yet a slightly different form are manifestations of an unhealed mind. They come to you not to make you miserable, but because you have asked them to, so that you can relive what was once a movie of victimization and have it changed to a movie of forgiveness. This is easily accomplished if you allow me to take charge of the dream and place it in your awareness where it can be seen merely as a dream. Yet so often you simply do not ask! And so you replay the darkened nightmare as if it were a real threat, and so you respond to it with fear and anger instead of Love.

Love cannot come where you will not allow it. And pain and anger is but a way you protect your heart and mind from further damage. Unfortunately, this makes the nightmare all the more real. The population is living their lives in a constant nightmare! And they have learned to accept it as "just the way it is perceived!"

How unfortunate are they who will not have their pain, guilt and suffering removed by God from their minds! This is God's only wish: that you may let your dreams go and wake up with Him holding your hand, lifting you high into blissful Heaven.

Yet Heaven cannot come into an unforgiven mind. And what you hold back for yourself interferes with Christ's helping Hand. Wherever you still find hatred and the unforgiving welcome to guard you or protect you somehow, you have given your power to a relentless ego that seeks with every turn a way in which to make you suffer more. Would you want any of this knowing that your Father does not even acknowledge it! He cannot see what is a dream or a nightmare because God IS REAL. What is real does not delve into anything else. It doesn't need to. Nor do you little child! Nor do you.

Give all your agreements to the Holy Spirit to be transformed by Love. This will always help you to follow through with total commitment, because you will be glad by the lasting happiness it brings.

Use time to have the Holy Spirit help undo your any need for it. The Holy Instant waits in eternity there for you. Join with all brothers and sisters there where true joining is all that is possible.

For unity is God's Creation and not yours. You cannot control your creation, but merely live within the framework God has placed within it. If you live to know and have only the truth, only this will find you. But if you make up reality as you would have it be, or, think it should be, you must suffer.

Guilt cannot find a home on a clean and shiny mirror. But you will see yourself in it, if you take the time needed to clean the dust off. Darkness, guilt and hatred are the dusts of fear. Leave them on their own and they will completely cloud your reflection of your Self. You can hold a shiny mirror if you look for only truth and peace in your friends. Leave your agenda behind and let God's Agenda replace it.

Christ will lead you both to a place where only light is present because only light is desired. And since only light truly exists, you ask for a treasure that is truly forever yours. As you awaken in this field of treasure, you will awaken with other angels who look only to find God's light within you. They too have learned to be without conditions. Their agenda is present and clear because there are no secrets in the Home of Heaven.

Ask each one you meet to join you where you both live together in Heaven. Remember little child, you would be best to never think on your own. Ask for loving guidance with all thoughts, and realize that your enduring protection lies only there!

ON
COUNSELING
AND
MINISTRY

This section addresses one of your most important issues: faith.

You can read the words in this material and feel good for a while. Or, you can read these words and act upon them and live them and feel good for all eternity.

Many will do the first. It's God's Will, however, that you do the second. How many will read and disregard His Will within a few moments? The answer is many. The reason is because you all are so trained and conditioned to act from fearful instead of loving impulses that it is second nature to you. You need desperately to retrain your minds to live in light and love and peace. Many may see this as if I am trying to take candy from a child. However, in this case, it is not candy. Rather, it is a great weapon of self-destruction.

When you minister or counsel another it is your responsibility to merely love and accept them. They cannot learn from only words. That is why I am explaining to you that you must put these words into action. Love is not idle. Love is always inclusive, truly helpful, positive action. However, loving action is often not a matter so much of doing, as it is a matter of truly sharing.

True sharing is unconditional in its giving and does not entail the giving of things, necessarily. To minister to another, the minister is first required to awaken herself. She is awakened by her gifts of love to others. The gift of Love does not cost because it is attitudinal rather than physical. There is never a cost for the genuine gift of Love. Its essence is your own soul. But, you need to remember your soul so you become helpful to another's remembering.

There is no one alive who is not counseling or ministering some form of dogmatic practice. If you are practicing alcohol or drug abuse, that is what you are ministering and trying to teach in the present. That is why you should question every form of teaching before you accept it for your own by asking the Spirit within you to decide for you in every new situation. It takes only a moment for the Holy Spirit to answer for you, and you will know it is His Answer by the attitude that follows.

Everyone is a counselor, teacher and minister. Without exception there is no one who is not practicing one or more of the three. However, be sure that you know what the true teacher of God entails.

It is not my words any more than it is someone else's words, that each of you are searching for. Far be it. For words do not offer real experience unless they lead constantly away from fear and have the holy effect of joining hearts and minds in total peace. When this truly occurs the Holy Spirit has indeed spoken. The peaceful attitude that God's Messenger leads you to is unmistakable and eternally real. This Message is the miracle.

The other side of receiving counseling or ministry is careful listening and keeping an open mind. You should practice this every moment you are awake. To do so will lead to lasting awakening which is the meaning of the rapture the Bible speaks of.

Be still and know that you are God. There is no exception to this statement. For in genuine stillness will you find your Creator. And nowhere else will He be found. Not in dogma. Not in religious beliefs or any belief for that matter.

Remember: whatever you teach so shall you learn. There is no exception to this. Peace is never loud and is surely not dependent of the engagement of intellectualism or the pursuit of scholars. It is discovered when the tools of the ego are completely overlooked and then exchanged for a quiet and peaceful light in love.

God is exuded through the peaceful to those still searching for peace. And in this genuine gentleness that you would offer they will awaken next to you. And they will gladly exchange their worldly motives for the miracle once they experience the miracle with you. And so is the world vanished, gone back to being what it always was: nothing at all.

You do not realize how desperate you are for the joy of nothingness. You seek it in every activity. You believe that if you just do this or that, you will feel the peace of not having to think or act. You have worn yourselves out believing that if you just do one more something you will finally remember there is nothing to do.

Everything in Heaven is done. So is it done on earth. The end of the world is already come, and you just don't see it yet. When you counsel or minister to another keep the enlightened idea in mind that the world is gone and Heaven is come right now! Fear not the counsel to the end of the world. It truly is come and you do dwell now in Heaven dear ones!

ON
WILLINGNESS

You have the willingness to work hard, to raise your families, to play and fight, to build and destroy, to take birth and experience physical death, to use and abuse yourself and others and basically make a place of once peace into a complex and dark world.

The ego has a willingness to do anything in its power to keep you from true peace and God. Your urge to fix everything you look upon is often relentless. You cannot accept that peace may be available to you in the blink of an eye merely by changing the focus to within.

So often you are all so busy building illusions and delusions that you most often fail miserably to do what God has destined for you: to forgive and forget the world entirely and remember Heaven. Had you learned long ago that peace is your only true goal, you would not be facing the dilemma now that your unhealed history has brought to you in the present.

There are tears in Heaven for you who have not been able to truly forgive and join again together as God has so willed. Yet as humanity, you are still given time to do just this. You have no real idea of how much you need the one or ones you see as "enemy." They are your brothers and sisters. And they are as much a part of you as God and Heaven!

You need to have one kind of willingness kept in conscious awareness at all times: how to be truly helpful and inclusive in your willingness to help others.

You do not judge the one who has assaulted another as "bad." You also do not judge the one who has given more to others as "better." Simply put, you do not judge because you cannot judge. All of God's children are deserving of acceptance and love because they are God's children. There is no exception to this statement because this is God's One Will.

Your will is always at work. Your willingness merely follows your will. You cannot escape will because it is built into your creation. Yet you can will for things that will hurt your experience rather than help it. Again, this is why you should always ask before proceeding with an action. Do your best to align your will with the loving Will of our Father in Heaven.

Ask first! I will answer with His Decision for you. There is never a time in which Christ is not at your side. Never! So ask first and then listen to His loving Answer. The answer may not appease you, but it is always right because it is Heaven's Decision and not yours alone. And what is Heaven but a state of life and mind that could never hurt you? You dwell here but do not see it, only because you have exchanged it for something else the ego sees as more appealing. How insane the ego must be to choose pain and suffering over peace and complete happiness!

The dream you see as your physical reality you call your world. Yet what is your world except your will-ingness to accept it, define it and speak of it as others have taught you from their own past. And if the past is not real, and I assure you it is not, then how do you really define what you think you see? The truth is that you can't, at least not in any meaningful way. And so if your agreed definitions are not really meaningful why would you bother? You bother because it is the ego's way of maintaining the illusion that you are separate from your Creator.

The ego calls its definitions not only meaningful, but essential. It calls on you to accept its word as the true authority. And thus, it tells you that all you survey has meaning, definition and value. And you have bought this darkened plan hook, line and sinker.

Why do you not question its value? Could it be the ego fears its own death and will do anything to persuade you that through its definitions it keeps you alive? But you must ask the ego this question: "Is this really my life in only this world I perceive?" The ego is confused by this question because it does not really know. And so, it will avoid answering by guiding you to think of something else, regarding the question as insane.

Yet ask your heart honestly, and God's spirit will come to remind you that heaven is your only home. And the detour you have accepted as a path to life has simply forsaken you, for there is no life in fear or any perceptions that may tempt you to believe otherwise.

Practice to have the willingness to not see the world as home. It is not. And nothing that seems to happen in the world can ever hurt you. Understand this totally and our Home you will remember!

ON
RIGHT
AND
WRONG

In defining right from wrong it is very simple: what is loving and kind is always right.

What is unloving is always wrong. Yet being wrong does not constitute any sort of punishment or retaliation. This is merely the world's upside down decision: an eye for an eye. Those who make unloving decisions in your regard are calling for help, and for the love and acceptance they can't find with you. You must thus decide for them and not against them. When you choose love for them you are acting on the Holy Spirit's Decision for both of you.

The Heart of Compassion is God's Heart in you. You can learn to reflect this Heart, and you must, for miracles to occur. Miracles are what you need and all you need because Love is all you have forgotten.

Without your brothers and sisters, you would have no means of expressing the miracle. Without each other there would be no means for discovering the meaning of joy. The very meaning of joy is to share what is real for both of you. The common traits of the ego cannot be shared because they are not unanimous and have varying results without real and genuine consistency.

Right decisions are always a reflection of the willingness to be humble and true in the Presence of God. You cannot experience humility and true gentleness without stepping away from your own attraction to judge. The ego equates God with a stormy judgmental figure because it does not understand true authority.

True authority has no need to judge because God knows His Creation is not apart from its Source. God cannot judge what He created. Why would He? If Creation is like the Father in every way, then what would be the use? Only if what God created is a mistake would He need to judge. Anyone who has any common sense at all must realize instantly the futility of what is Perfect judging Itself!

That is why whenever you judge another you are belittling yourself and God. Anyone who belittles must believe in arrogance rather than gentle grandeur, for they cannot know their own greatness because they fail to experience it in their sisters and brothers. This failure is merely a decision to look upon yourself and others with the darkened filters the ego presents first.

At this point it is up to you whether or not you will gracefully choose to overlook the sight this judgment presents. Or, mistakenly decide to look upon another with the dark filters the ego has made to present to you its picture of delusion and separation.

The appearances made of the physical are merely false attractions to preoccupy your mind with fear instead of the choice to occupy your heart and mind with only love.

The decision to overlook the physical is found only in the Holy Instant. This instant contains the seed of the light from Heaven that you both are searching for. How is peace and joining with another in God's presence possible without the timelessness Heaven offers in this holy step out of time?

Where God lives, out of time and in His eternal Heaven, so do you live while merely dreaming. Heaven is easily within your reach because there is no distance really separating you. The distance you seem to see is but a physical projection of measurement that you have learned in the world's schoolroom. Yet there is no measurement between you and God. And so, there is no measurement separating you from any brother or sister.

The assessments I have given you above are right assessments because of the direction they would lead you. I am leading you away from the world of fear and guilt so that you can find your happiness. There is no happiness in time. You will find no peace in a world where opposites are given equality. The opposite of joy is a deluded mind that gives credence to time. This mind will search and search and never reach its goal. It is hell. And hell has many beliefs and perceptions none of which have any meaning or value. You can easily escape this all through the practice of non-judgment.

What has value comes from love, gives love and returns to love. What is opposite to love is simply not here and is therefore unworthy of your attention. Replace the unworthy by allowing the Holy Spirit to fill your heart with His Love. Connect with this love by giving it to others, always. Know His abundance as the love you came to share. Do your little part by letting only love work through you, for you and with you. Be still, and know that you are indeed Love.

ON

JESUS
AND
WORSHIP

I do not ask for your worship toward me, but for only the Father above.

I deserve your honor, respect and your willingness to truly listen when I answer, for I am merely a brother who has gone before you and therefore knows the way. I have forgiven all mankind without exception, and so when you fail to forgive on some level, I will always offer a mild and gentle hand to lift you back to Heaven.

You obviously do not believe you are in Heaven because your mind is clouded by such bad dreams. The very fact that you believe you can actually think without God is so preposterous that you have badly frightened yourself with the making of the darkened world you see.

Even unto death you believe the world is sacred and will be so sorely missed that you weep at the very thought of leaving it behind. You cherish the place your body lives and yet you often regret ever being born into such a place.

Is this not madness, little child? You fear Heaven and yet you also fear the world. You cling so hard to the world believing that Heaven may only be a little better. Yet you must let go. Be it now or be it right before the body dies away, you must eventually let go of your firm grasp to the physical.

I tell you, Do this now so that you can be free. Hold on to nothing but the light you already are, for in this act of trust you will fly in freedom to your Creator. You need only let go of dream of thought and thus the dream of the world. It is not hard. It is as natural as the light from which you came!

You ask how you should worship and yet you then decide for yourself by worshipping the world anyway. You ask to come to God empty handed, but then you try to drag your wagon of gold and silver chalices behind you. You say you do not want the world, but then the hunger comes and you take it all back again. It is very hard for you each to decide. That is why you should always ask in every situation for me to decide for you.

In every decision I can equip your heart and mind with the reminder to forgive and act upon it. When you fail in completing this it is simply because you have chosen not to listen and to decide for yourself alone. Yet in your decision alone you can never be happy. You will not know true joy until you ask the Holy Spirit to release you on behalf of God and His Heaven. When you ask truly you will know again that you are free. But do not ask with your ego, for the ego must only deceive. And you will wonder why you did not hear His Gentle Answer.

I do not ask that you worship my body in any form. Do not look upon me as one who has suffered, but only as one who has been forgiven, is forgiven and has forgiven and is therefore redeemed with all mankind.

Take my redemption freely for it is my one gift of innocence and total freedom from sin and guilt that I offer you now. It is only the Gift of God I would share with you. Ask for only this and you will receive only this, and Heaven will be smiling and shining through you.

It does not matter what religion you cling to. I transcend all religion so that you may rise above all differences with me. You need not even call me by name, for every angel in Heaven knows I AM.

There is no man or woman alive who does not carry my spirit within themselves. I am literally a part of you and not separate in any way. In your recognition that we are indeed truly joined is your genuine escape from the world and all forms of fear.

When the world does end, will you know where your life really belongs? Will you find safety in what truly belongs to you, or merely in what you seem to own for a short while? Eternal Life is the only safe bet. And for those who haven't figured this out, they are free to keep looking in other places. Yet they take the long and harsh road home. And this need not be. For eternal Life is simple when you don't fight against it. And the rewards by far outlast all that you see and now think to hold onto.

Only God is truly yours. Only God is what you truly want. Only God's Love can last for you, and nothing else will.

You who ask God only for peace for yourselves and for your sisters and brothers will surely find it. For only Heaven can provide this truly. And it is no distance to travel to find it. All you must do is ask and ask truly. Not one problem you have is but already solved. Nothing in the world around you can ever hurt you. What you truly have forever can never be taken from you. The joy God took in creating you is everlasting. Be vigilant to remember what is only truly everlasting, for in this formula alone are you truly free! I AM everlasting life. In me is the freedom, the life you seek.

ON
FORGIVENESS

You do not need belief in any dogma, religion or any particular way of life that would or could be categorized and defined if you learn how to truly forgive.

God does not charge Himself with religion. Yet since He created you in perfect light and love you must practice release from all that would not fit into the perfection of Heaven.

You are therefore charged with the responsibility and task of learning to forgive since this is the only way back to the peace of God and Heaven. Those who do not or cannot forgive are merely charged with only the monotony of a world they themselves made to replace their Father's Heaven.

And if only all they see and hear is real, where is Heaven for them? They have excluded themselves from joy, peace and happiness by their own misplaced decision to be selfish and insecure. They have become takers instead of givers, users instead of lovers, and warriors instead of peace seekers. They call constantly for you to join their ranks, advertising in every way and at every corner possible for your "voluntary commitment." Yet what they teach is no more voluntary than it is natural. Hatred and scorn is their way, for they have lost their sanity and their own connection with the one loving God. It is to those who are lost whom God sends His miracle workers. Which company would you join?

To learn forgiveness truly is a total commitment. You cannot forgive one making him an angel while holding a grudge towards another making him into a devil. Salvation does not work that way, nor will it ever. God forgave His entire Creation the moment when a part of it forgot Him, merely by not recognizing the mistake that was made. And so must you learn again to over-look the cloud that is not really in the way of the sun.

The Son shines through even though darkness does its best to invade the light. But light always overcomes, and shines through to everyone because it is genuine and real. That is why each shall know Him when He comes. There is no doubt when true light and happi-ness arise within you and extend to all. Surely, in this holy joining you will remember.

There is a false forgiveness to condemn and a real forgiveness to heal. Forgiveness to condemn is preten-tious and says, "I will forgive you this time even though you are undoubtedly a miserable sinner as am I." While forgiveness to heal merely recognizes instantly that the error never really occurred for either of you.

You may believe it is hard to forgive with true forgive-ness. Yet I assure you this is not the case. It is hard for the ego because the ego is so dedicated to the past and future that it cannot allow itself to enter into any light. And it is much harder to maintain the illusion of hatred and condemnation because it is so unnatural. You are not asked to heal the ego perception; I will do this for you with God's Help. Merely step out of darkness and take my hand and I will lift you from the misguided and fearful thinking of the ego.

Forgiveness never looks upon errors making them real and then pretending to forgive them. The ego, however, does, and does it well. And it will pretend while saving its hatred for a later occasion when another error or even greater mistake is seen. Then it will pounce pronouncing to you, "I told you so!" The ego always looks for mistakes, particularly physical ones which have absolutely no value, and when corrected have no real meaning. This sets up a situation that becomes entirely unfixable in ego terms because the illusion that an attempt for correction is made does not exist in the first place.

God's Holy Spirit never corrects the physical because it is a waste of time. He goes right to the source, which is only the mind. By succeeding here He releases you from the burden of guilt and danger and gently reminds the mind and heart that it does not matter, returning it to the present and freeing you instantly from your past errors.

The ego, on the other hand, wants you to pay dearly for every past error and will incarcerate both the body and the mind with as many forms of guilt and punishment as it can find and justify. Your decision, no matter how small, to side with the ego is indeed insane. And the results of this choice make it necessary for time to be extended so that forgiveness can once again be re-found. Yet you do not want time. Every minute of isolation is wasted instead of helping to save one another.

God is not your savior, for He has never really lost His sons and daughters. You, however, are your brother's and sister's savior, for they need you as much as you need them. Let each remind you of the Help that you both must need.

The world must indeed be healed together without exception, for Heaven is not separate from anyone without exception. You will not heal with religion, spirituality or any form of education. You will heal simply with God's own simple Light. Your dogma, religious beliefs and other philosophies cannot bring you Home. The light-hearted shall enter Heaven because they have simply and without exception accepted God and his own simple truth: I AM the light of the world and the world does not exist. Remember this simple phrase and take it to heart and practice it in every situation and you will discover Heaven and be free.

ON
MEDITATION
AND PRAYER

In every prayer there is an underlying request.

The request can be for things, for thoughts, or for mere help in changing one's mind. True prayer is for help in changing one's mind, instead of getting what a person thinks they need physically. When you pray for something physical, it is a statement in itself that you believe you are somehow lacking. Everyone has times in life when they feel poor in body and in soul.

Yet true prayer requires that one ask for spiritual help and not physical help. If you need some form of physical help, however, prayer is indeed a helpful tool, and God will not deny you. He will send forth an angel in disguise to assist you. Understand that God never denies you of anything. You deny yourself, but only because you feel incapable or unworthy somehow.

True prayer is for-*giving* and not for-*getting*. If you will remember this always, it will facilitate a space for healing to enter into your own awareness. Pray to remember what you already have and are, and not for things that cannot truly help you. Remember that you are created whole as well as complete, and that imagined needs are a form of Self-denial. When you believe you are lacking you cannot be thinking with God's Holy Spirit.

Pray for remembrance of your wholeness first, and upon this recognition you will be fulfilled from within, and then given the awareness necessary for the complete wholeness to manifest in your affairs.

Remember that prayer is fulfilled only through light. Without light, prayer could not be completed. Where there is light, darkness disappears, and with it, so do all forms of belief in lack. Light attracts abundance, and so your brothers and sisters who share this light will come to surround you. This sounds like magic, but I assure you, this is miraculous!

Those who see themselves as not whole or incomplete, that is, as if to be miserable sinners who lack in all regard, need your enlightened assurance to awaken them. They see themselves encumbered by all sorts of limitation and lack. They sicken themselves through their strong belief in guilt, fear and finally, hell.

You may think you have for the most part transcended these lower beliefs. Yet I assure you that as long as one person roams the world with a personal belief in lack and limitation, you stand next to him, never above him.

If you would be so happy in your enlightenment you must walk with him hand and hand. Those who believe they walk behind or ahead of another brother or sister are merely fooling themselves by allowing their own ego to disguise their anger and hatred into a seemingly joyful scene.

This is why your prayers must first be inclusive entirely. When you meditate, keep everyone you know within the invisible circle with you. Abundance is for everyone. If it were any different it would not be abundance, but something else disguised in darkness as abundance.

When you pray for some thing, remember: God has already given you everything. If you have not received the gifts you believe you need, then you have accepted a belief of unworthiness about yourself and, or about others.

You need nothing because everything is already yours. You find this hard to believe only because you have accepted the limited and dark picture of yourself that the ego has presented to you. Do not believe any part of this picture! You made this picture from earlier learned beliefs that at the time were thought to protect you somehow. Let them all go.

You are unlimited in capability because your own presence is the same Presence of God. If you do not view yourself through the Holy Spirit's unlimited view, only you can decide to have it changed. It is so simple and instantaneous a decision, you need but blink and there it is.

At one time, perhaps when you were very young, you did this naturally. You did not judge it or think about it, you simply changed your mind, stopped your current thinking, and allowed Love to carry you on to the next playground. Do you remember this, little child?

You should. It is the magic in your soul that you were created truly of. It has never left you, and awaits you to own its power again. Use this simplicity as you did so easily and miraculously when you were young. And now, be young again! It is my blessing upon you to share our innocence together. Let no one or no thing take this again from you. This is my gift today to you. Accept it in joyous tears. Truly by God, it is yours forever!

ON
LOVE AND JOY

What may you find together if most of you shift your goals to peace and giving instead of war and getting?

If you choose the inner world of love as reality you will automatically deny the illusion that seems outside you. You will first experience a kind of "spiritual amnesia" that will cause you to overlook the world and all perception and choose an instant of holiness with everyone you meet.

The emotional and spiritual will begin to outweigh the analytical and logical. You will come to depend more on connecting with everyone in a light and loving moment instead of standing back in judgment and remaining analytical.

Whatever purpose you are involved with may seem to become trivial at first. But as you adjust, you will connect to others in a more meaningful way. You will not be so dependent on words, but more on the silence between the words, the place where hearts are joined.

You will be less likely to argue and most likely to agree because you will realize the lack of validity the world and its apparent substance are made from. You will not define as you notice it becomes a wasted effort. Instead, you will try to slip past the trivial and material conversations you once enjoyed with others.

Getting will be replaced by giving. And at some point you will truly realize the world does not exist for you any longer, at least not in the way you once overvalued. You will cry some at first, but then you will begin to laugh more than cry. You will not feel fulfilled by any action of the world, but by your decision to be truly helpful in service to others.

If you succeed in your goal of forgiving others and the world of illusion that seems outside you, you will lighten so that you may feel as though you are flying. You are beginning your journey into the heart and back to Heaven!

Be vigilant for Heaven and not the world! Train your minds to overlook all judgment and perception and join instead with the Holy Spirit of Love in others. This is God's Will for you. I represent God's Will because I have come before you as Christ His Son. I am therefore one with the part of your mind that remains still in Heaven. Make no mistake. You are entirely safe while sleeping and dreaming—you are elsewhere. Yet it is now useless to do so since I have taken your hand.

You believe in me even though your ego disagrees. Be willing to take whatever disagrees and give it to me so I can remove it with the Holy Spirit's help from your mind forever! Do not allow the part of your mind that thinks you are thinking to rule your One Life any longer.

God's Thought is your only Reality and there are no words in Heaven. In Heaven you are joined with every sister and brother and everyone without exception.

Happiness is serene, and only gentleness can come out of your relationships with others. Will you not join with me here? I am waiting in your heart to take you home to Heaven. You may keep your body for a while but do not worship it or any of the world around you.

Most of all, practice overlooking your own thinking and the thinking of others. If a brother or sister asks you to do something or listen, do so, whether you agree or not.

Every one who comes to you calls out for their salvation. Would you not give it with a smile of acceptance from Heaven?

Love and joy are your only reality because they are only God's Reality. Anything else is illusory, a curtain of fear and anger you have made to hide from the truth in you. You do not want its coldness and darkness any longer! Give it to me for good and forever and be reborn into the light you came from!

I have said I have come as a light into the world. What I meant was that the light and the world could never be joined. How could what does not exist be joined with anything or anyone?

I am the light of the world with You. Never doubt this for it is but a doubting of God. God has no doubt. You are all His children and no matter how your ego tries this cannot be changed. You are free to fight against it as long as you wish, however, everyone gets tired and gives up at some point. You are giving up nothing and gaining everything in return! The world and Heaven can never be reconciled because one of the two does not exist. I need not remind you that it is not Heaven. Be still and listen, for you will hear the Heart of Heaven in you. Accept His Gift as your own and now be free.

ON
FAITH

Your faith is ongoing and never ceases.

Everyone always trusts in something or someone all of the time. Your trust and faith should always be in Love because you are as God is: perfect Love. By trusting only Love you trust everyone without exception because Love is your real identity. Your true being-ness is not individualized, which you find hard to accept.

When you say, "I do not trust that person," you are merely saying you do not trust in God for yourself or him or anyone. Faith is an all or nothing decision. You cannot have partial faith in anything or anyone. You can, however, have faith in others without holding faith in their ego.

The common mistake of placing faith in other's egos instead of Christ is easily withheld if you learn to overlook physicalness entirely. The physical choice always combines with subtle or obvious conditions and strange agreements that bind each individual with contracts based in the promotion of fear and guilt.

The illusion of a whole world was built in this framework. Yet the framework is merely made of straw, and never reaches past the meaningless darkness it was formed from.

Creation is One and it is that simple. What seems separate is merely and simply illusion. You are always communicating with your Self and that is all. It is when you do not believe this that you are apt to cross into a fearful and isolating state. This state of mind is faithless and does not exist. It weaves many paths that all lead only to an infinite and useless search. You need not search. Merely have faith in the larger Self that is often hidden from you by your fears and guilt. The fact that *you think* you think promotes only a false awareness that can never last. It is the body's perception and not your Home.

You cannot fight fear and guilt because it is self-fulfilling by the very act of attempting to fight it. You believe in its presence because you made it and nothing more. Yet this is not your creation though it seems to be. It is but an etheric dream and that is all.

All that is truly creative in you remains in your true Reality. You cannot see or touch it because it is already part of you. There are no boundaries in your creation because eternity contains everything and lacks nothing.

Yet the everything I refer to is not physical. This is why great faith is required. Faith must exceed the physical to be true. With belief, you must have seen some past image. With faith, the image is overlooked and experience becomes paramount.

To experience Reality you merely slip out of time through the action of forgiveness by overlooking all that the senses tell you. The treasure, though unseen, is felt as true freedom and inner warmth. It is unmistakable because it is as pure as it is real. You will not fail to discover it children, because your heart is kept within its cove. Nothing threatens it because it is the Home of God!

How easy it is to shift your faith from the world to Heaven! It is as natural as awakening from a dream. It is as pure and gentle as a baby's smile. It is as warm as a joyous mother's arm. It is unmistakable because it exceeds all the world could offer. It is my promise to you, for you are indeed safe and saved.

Do not forget the importance of applying genuine forgiveness to everyone and everything without exception. This is your key in the cessation of thinking. And Knowledge will follow with God's full promise of a pure and enlightened blessing.

Welcome Home, gentle brother and sister! Your long trip soon comes to an end with a new beginning that has never ceased and has always been. You can stop thinking now. It is okay to walk through Heaven's door. No guilt shall follow. No fear shall enter this Place with you. The walls of light protect you, for indeed, you are Home! Have faith, thus, only in Heaven.

ON

SIN

Everyone who comes here "misses the mark."

In this sense everyone has sinned. It is a forgetting of God while making a decision. Every one who has come here has forgotten God at one time or another. I am no exception, but learned through my complete change of mind to choose only gentleness in even the most extreme of cases. My ministry is to teach you and remind you of our inner perfection.

Missing the mark or "sinning" is part of the human condition because you made it this way by accepting laws not made by God. The world is not God's any more than your body is your own. The body belongs to the ego, for it was made as a symbol for the separation from God.

The separation from Love, indeed, seems real to you. You made it this way, but only to help lead you home. You cannot gauge how steadily you walk on the path Home without acknowledging the tripping on the stones as well. Everyone who has come here has detoured from the path of enlightenment onto a road full of fear. The real question is: how will you handle it when you fumble along the way? Will you ask me to lead you home?

You have been taught very early in your earthly life that punishment is the result for those who stray from both God's Law and man's. You came to earth and forgot God. In the same instant you were designated from your own rebirth to remember. To remember God is your only purpose here. Sin is merely a forgetting of this holy purpose. To fulfill your purpose you must learn how to forgive.

True forgiveness is received the moment it is recognized that your mistakes could never really hurt you, and therefore never really occurred. Eternal Love cannot be harmed or destroyed or punished in any form. All that has ever seemed to hurt you are merely your failures to forgive and receive God's Love. As you grow, your failures will indeed lessen because you will eventually find that learning in this way is quite limited. No one can learn harmlessness from hurtfulness. Yet they can learn to correctly identify what it is they truly want and need.

You must learn with full dedication to teach love in every situation. And you will succeed because God's Will surpasses every other.

If each person comes here to heal his or her hatred and sense of separation (and I assure you, you do) then how many more lifetimes must it take if you are punished in the one you are in? Bringing this one awareness to you is the whole purpose of this material! One sin only links its chain to another and another sin. When forgiveness replaces the link, then the chain is broken.

Punishment makes evil and darkness more real, making it more attractive and powerful for you to abide by the laws of punishment instead of the eternal law of innocence you are created by.

You may vacillate between the ideas of sinfulness and innocence for a while. Forgiveness is a practice; while knowing Creation is a state arising from true forgiveness. Time is given to you for this purpose. Do not waste a moment giving into any form of hatred or angered opposition. Overlook all opposition by gently forgiving first. By doing so the need for judgment is overcome.

The miracle occurs with the smallest willingness to forgive. Here, a change of heart and mind are indeed possible. Help your brothers and sisters achieve this change by not judging. By doing so you allow the

Spirit of Love to extend through you and into the Self you share with everyone. In this choice you will soon recognize that all minds and hearts are joined both in purpose and in creation.

Two hearts and minds joined as one conveys the experience of holiness to all. And everyone will recognize this holy joining by the light that emanates from this one purposeful gathering of two of more. It cannot be denied by even the angriest, for they, too, will easily submit to what is forever real and life giving. In this shared innocence is God recognized and shared. You live for this experience, and indeed, you will find and achieve it!

Perhaps here is a simpler way to understand sin:

Sin is the decision to see without God. Everything seen through the vision of God is holy and wholly true. Everything else is seen with perception, which is not true, which is a mistake or sin, which are the same.

Everyone who has come here has made a decision to see through perception, which has given power to judgment and the desire for specialness, substituting holiness for sin. Sin is merely a mistaken thought, which can only be healed through forgiveness, which leads to salvation. Salvation is seen only with the vision of God and Christ, who are eternally joined as One. Your Self remains in this Oneness, a fact you have often been apt to forget.

Sin is experienced in time; holiness is experienced in eternity.

Sin is experienced in time because of your temptation to follow a voice you made apart from God. You do not want this voice; holiness is experienced in eternity, and is the Voice of both gentle silence and sureness, bringing only a true sense of your own safety and joy.

The Holy Instant gives us an instant of eternity and an experience of holiness. In this experience of holiness all sin, all mistakes fall away and you experience the peace of God.

Any experience in which the peace of God is not present, any thought in which we do not experience the total peace of God, is a mistake or a sin, which are the same. Yet sin can never really hurt you because of its natural falsity. It doesn't exist, and you will only know this when you allow forgiveness to rest upon it.

Sin is a mistaken thought and because it is mistaken it can and will be corrected, because it is the Will of God and Christ, which is our own Will. God's Will and Christ's Will are the same.

God's only vision is perfect Love. Perception, which is a mistake, (or sin) sees only hate, many times disguised as Love. The "love" that comes from perception is always hatred in disguise no matter what form it seems to take, and no matter how loving it is perceived to be because it is only perception, and it is not the experience of truth.

The truth is only Love. It has no perception; it only loves. It sees only love. It is only love. It extends only love. Truth creates through love and extends love through God and Christ, as co-creators. Love creates only love.

Sin makes only perception, often multi-layered and repressed, which you must give to His Light. Sin is a mistaken thought that the Holy Spirit, which is one with your true Self, will correct this perception through your willingness. There is no other way. Any other attempt is a procrastination in time, to maintain and perpetuate the need for more time.

Your only function here is to give your perceptions to the Holy Spirit, which is your true Self, for correction that leads you to the vision of God. And God will take the final step with your true willingness to bring your mind home to Christ where we all truly abide together and forever.

What is the purpose of sin? Sin calls out for Love to come into your heart and into the world when the Holy Spirit is given full charge of healing the nature of sin, which is only "false love." To heal the mind that believes in sin is to give the false sense of self, the ego or illusion to the truth and awareness of Love.

Love melts away the perception of sin and brings healing to the mind that believed its judgments to be real and "helpful." Truly helpful words and actions stem from your own awareness of God's Love. Only Love is truly helpful.

The only purpose of sin is for its undoing, although hidden in the ego's agenda it becomes a form of weaponry harming everyone's awareness of peace.

The only true function that will bring peace to your mind and everyone's mind is the decision of willingness to forgive all of our mistaken thoughts and we exchange this sin of mistaken thoughts for God's Love. When the mind makes this decision to exchange sin with the Love the Holy Spirit always offers, which is our true nature, it is shared through the entire son-ship.

There is no sin in peace.

ON
LOSS

You who live within the seeming boundaries of an illusory world mostly equate loss with people and things you hold dear.

Yet this should be a constant reminder to you that the illusion of loss could never be real. What God creates can never be lost, and what seems lost never really is. It is this simple. And so any thing or one that seems lost to you is but a part of your own self-made fearful dream. The eternal does not die. And what is not eternal does not matter. It never really existed, except in dreams.

You seem to feel loss at times because the ego, and not the Holy Spirit, is leading you. You are merely listening to the wrong voice, and then, equating loss with a false reality.

You see it as real only because you are falsely dependent on your illusions and dreams. They can be many, made of bodies, things and other false idols. But their attraction is clearly an indication of your sense of separation from Love. How could this be except by cherishing only the physical and forgetting about the miracle that patiently awaits you?

The physical offers nothing but dreams that must fade into more and more loss, until you are willing to look upon the world and the physical differently. And this requires merely a shift in perception for you.

True perception always leads to the Heart of Love in you and your brother and sister. Always. If you do not feel love, it is because you have decided against reality and for delusions, illusions and special false dependencies. As special as these illusions may seem to you, they can never last because you made them without love.

Heaven is not special. It is your Reality. It is therefore real and very holy, and, you cannot change it. Look therefore for only the changeless in yourself and others. The light is only there. But its grandeur is indeed immense. For it is in everyone you see, past his or her frightening dreams and false dependencies.

See this and only this in others and the Spirit of Love will teach you how best to respond to everything and everyone. It is the one lesson you came to learn because it is the only lesson you came to complete. It is why you came here. It is your redemption and return to holiness.

You will either learn pain from loss or you will remember God by it. By learning truly of God you will remember that you can lose nothing.

By remembering this and keeping always close to your heart, you will learn of your own invulnerability, and, the invulnerability of everyone. Help is always given to those who recognize their own invulnerability because they are asking the right Source. They would choose real freedom instead of attachment and specialness.

Thus, you have been given life to rediscover. And this you will remember in the end. There is no way you cannot learn it in the end, simply because the end is given you to remember the Beginning. Do not sway your eyes away from this happy lesson. You have nothing to fear by embracing it fully as God has asked you.

Take heart in your own inner Abundance, for it has never failed you, though you have often failed to rely on only it. For in this equation is your real and full awakening. When this lesson is truly received you will reveal it to the world and never look back. It is your one destiny. It is your true calling. It is your full service to yourself and the whole of creation. It is your full and complete return to Love! And with each act of true forgiveness, you come still one step closer to your Goal.

The path I am asking you to follow is the path of least resistance, simply because I am asking you to merely give up the resistance you feel at times. The resistance more often than not tells you over and over again that loss is indeed real, and that you must always guard against it, placing you in the defensive and therefore in a state that is unloving to all.

You do not want this false sense of protection. It has limited you to only the physical, and it has kept you from your enlightenment. It has made you feel unworthy of the angels, God and Heaven. Is it worth this entirety, child? Indeed, if you look straight at what I am saying, you will discover that the answer is clearly no. Would God ever say yes to hell? He would not. And so should you be more careful to follow the Holy Spirit's lead home.

ON
ABUNDANCE
VERSUS
SCARCITY

In the world, the opposite of God seems to be real.

You value the valueless and cherish the cherishless. You seek comfort constantly in everything that is inconsistent. You love the unworthy and you hate the truly free. You are hardly a good teacher for anyone, including yourself. Yet you insist on making decisions all the time for everyone without your only Teacher's Help. Is this not quite strange?

You seem happy to fail at things over and over again, blaming yourself or others for your sense of inadequacy. Sometimes you get so angry you even blame God. Odd indeed! What is more, you continuously make the same mistakes, finally coming to such intense pain that you completely give up. The giving up is indeed wise! Why then, not practice this all the time? By doing so you will begin to abandon the ideals of scarcity and remember again how abundant you truly are.

Are the past and the future worth suffering so much for? Indeed, your suffering is in vain. You are merely wasting your free moments to indulge in a fantasy without meaning. And you must suffer while valuing the totally meaningless, for you are not free while you go on searching in dreams.

Everything is scarce to those who value but a dream and not reality. Abundance requires that you know thyself. You cannot believe in abundance, but you indeed can accept it and fully receive it.

Belief is an inappropriate response to Reality. God gave you Reality not to believe in, but to know. Belief is a sign you are not sure. Can God not be sure about His one Creation? He knows you as His created child who has never left Him.

True faith is you not believing because you are not sure, it is you believing because you have had the experience of knowing. God does not offer you concepts, ideas or beliefs. He offers the perfect joy of His remembrance. He knows you know Him and so you do. And indeed you must, whether you choose to believe or not. Belief does not matter.

Reality does not depend on faith or belief. It is real because God created it. It is that simple. Do you need to believe in love to love another? Of course not! You love her or you don't. And you do, even if you think you don't. Acceptance of this becomes the simple task at hand.

Your thinking is but the only thing standing between you and abundance. By overdepending on your own private thoughts you fail to recognize your Source, thus you fail to love, and lastly, you do not experience God's Gift to you.

His Gift is His joy and abundance. When you do not recognize God's Gift to you, you are merely replacing His Thought with your own. Your own thinking is love-less without the recognition of His great abundance within you. Without this recognition you are indeed lost to Christ, even though He stands right next to you waiting to retake your hand into God's Heart.

In His Heart is Christ waiting with all the loving abundance of all creation. His light is everywhere and is in everyone. Look only to this in your brother and sister and you will remember your own light that you forever share with them. How can there be lack where creation is recognized everywhere?

Every need you think you have is but a dream. You do not need to dream to achieve above merely surviving. You can achieve above survival simply by sharing. True sharing is a demonstration of your faith in yourself and others.

The immediate change from a scarce state of mind to an abundant and joyous state of mind is as simple as each new momentary inner decision. If you are in a scarce state of mind you are thinking about the past and future. In a joyous state you perceive nothing but the shining instant because this is your Reality as sure as you are life. It does not need your perception. It does not need justification or proof to anyone.

Yet Reality is instantly recognized as miraculous when others come in contact with it. It is true and everyone will know it. There is no doubt because of its Source. And angels surround you who quietly know and need not believe, for holiness is yours because God has given it to you and you have accepted it.

Humility comes naturally for anyone who remembers peace. Peace is the natural result for those who have asked and received only God's Gift. For what is His is yours forever and ever. And you will be happy with only this. Lack and scarcity are relative only to the ego, which cannot be reunited with God. Only the ego is lost and you need not follow it at all unless you wish to. It will help you stay unhappy if you do, and that is all.

ON
TIME AND
ETERNITY

We have spoken about the world and I have repeatedly stated in many different ways that the world of perception is made up and is therefore unreal.

You are not expected to believe this because you made it to take the place of reality. But you can remember eternity because it does not require perception or belief. When your perception is forgiven it will be healed.

Healing is all you who live in the world need be concerned with. You either choose to heal or hurt by your decision about the world and what you think it is for.

You made the world to take the place of eternity. And since you can only be happy when you remember eternity, then it is imperative that you forgive yourselves of all that you think, perceive and see. Since you are constantly tempted to look at the world as reality you must constantly retrain your minds to overlook what you now think is obvious to you.

What is obvious is only that you have made up a reality by your own made-up definitions and then forgot that you made it. You now believe that it is Creation, and to the extent that if it is denied of substance you will argue in every way imaginable to preserve your faith in it.

Yet I ask you this: what if the world is reality and Heaven but a dream? You have little to look forward to if you are not eternal, little child! And so you soon must decide between what the ego tells you is real and what I am gently attempting to show you. You will always have a choice. God gave you the power to decide and He will never take it away.

Yet for your own happiness I urge you now to sincerely begin to look upon the world much differently. You have made the world to stand between you and your Father. I ask you now, forgive and let the wall fall down. Let your heart be your guide and not your mistaken thinking. Waste not a moment in your decision to ask the Holy Spirit to remove your false perceptions so that you return to your own loving Freedom!

Every instant you are free from thought and misperception you experience the Holy Instant, which takes you further into eternity, into the experience of heaven and the presence of God.

You have been given time so that your belief in it can be gently undone. You will never be happy as long as you are a slave to it, such has the past proven. Will you not take my hand and leave the fear and guilt associated with the dream of time behind? What could be stopping you except an insanity that you still identify as "you?" It is not you. It is but a darkened dream without hope of salvation.

If time is real then eternity must be illusion. The ego proves this by attempting to convince you that since eternity cannot be measured then it must not exist. It counsels that time is linear and that since the past can be recorded the future will be as well. And what is recordable exists. A question must then arise. What is existence?

Existence depends on definition and the use of symbols. You would not know of existence without symbols, definitions and measurements. Without words to describe time you could not angrily remember the past or fear the future.

The whole thought system that made time was made from past visual measurements, mental separations and calculations and finally, words. Although not often, however, words can be used to lead away from past imprints, mental definitions and even words used to express their own temporary necessity and final undoing.

I am attempting to prepare you for just such an experience, because without symbols, definitions and words, your mind and heart will easily return to the loving presence of our Creator. Your own natural being-ness will simply take the place of the picture of existence you now see yourself in if what you are is led from dependency on the mind to a new and true dependency on the heart.

Your heart is defined as pure as God's Love because it is God's Love. You are much more immense than you can see, child of God's grandeur! The limits of the body are but illusions that with simple training you can easily transcend.

But you must leave the past and future to me entirely. You can still make future plans, but do not live in these plans or by them. Leave the future to what Love will bring to you next. It is that simple.

Keep your heart open and the mind will follow, rather than the heart following the mind. The mind is a terrifying leader. The heart is a minister to peace. Listen and know the difference.

Miracle workers are in short supply and in huge demand. Choose, then, to join with God and Christ on their mission to forget the world and remember Heaven. Ask the Holy Spirit in every decision and happiness cannot fail. Bringers of humility and true peace, be glad! Your return Home cannot fail. It is God's mission to have you remember and learn of heaven together.

ON

MIRACLES
AND
REVELATION

Contrary to common opinion, in seemingly dark days, there are miracles available for everyone.

But the work must be done without haste. For the masses turn their heads and look not joyously to strangers, fearing hurt and hatred. To those God sends His miracle workers, for those where darkness has seemingly overcome. The darkness cannot last. The light will overcome and all will remember for and with each other that truly they are sisters and brothers.

Without exception this will come to pass, for it is the Will of God that all shall celebrate Heaven together. What other will could God have but this? God is entirely merciful and calls to all to join Him in His holy mission for your remembrance of light. To do so is to recognize eternity and perfect freedom.

Punishment is reserved for only those who would hate, conquer and war. Yet God does not punish them. They punish themselves by believing in darkness, anger and hatred. They are confused, sometimes by the frightening concepts taught to them through anger in their youth.

Others have learned through rigorous training as adults because the hatred gives them a sense of power that they so strongly believe they lack. They have never learned to love gently as God loves them. They believe in conditions because they are conditioned, often by confused religious beliefs and sickened philosophies that can only bring about the need for more time to undo their sense of darkness, guilt and separation from Love.

God does not will such insanity on anyone! Without compromise, He Wills love for all and all for love without exception! He would not have destroyed what He Himself created.

And so those who would take lives take nothing. Yet they make the need for more lives so that they, too, can remember that only peace is the true way Home. This you each came to learn and remember. Until you accept this completely, you are bound in time to the same mistakes of others before you.

Yet a day will pass when the world will have fulfilled its only function: to give you each time to remember the holy and eternal truth of your one mission together here; to help one another and celebrate in love. This is not an idealistic dream. It is the Will of God and only Heaven is the result. Heaven is no dream, as soon you all will choose to remember. Together you will do this. I promise this to you. For I am with you leading you to our Home where we abide together, in the holiness of Heaven.

Every complete acceptance you offer your brother and sister is a miracle and leads everyone together back to Heaven. Any detour from this full acceptance leads to the need for more time to undo the fear it was made from. The detour usually takes the disguise of some form of distraction from the holy present.

And indeed the world has many, for it was made for the very purpose of disguising your Home from you. When you are tempted to take the things of the world and the world seriously, remember, there is a happier way. When you are distracted by the world's temptations, simply overlook them and turn inward to love with simple forgiveness.

You are not asked to look upon devastation and then overlook it. You are simply asked to overlook your own dreams of devastation! Merely reawaken from them by choosing Life instead of time. Time is as darkness is, as eternity is to light.

But where light has come, darkness disappears and so awakening becomes merely the recognition that for a moment you have forgotten that you are indeed at Home. You have slept and dreamt of hell, so much so that Heaven does not now seem possible. You may believe there is no escape from this darkness, but only because you have forgotten Who created you.

You did not make yourself, but you did make the world, as illusory and temporary as it must be. You cannot really change what you made because what was made to take the place of Heaven must be hell. Yet hell is so full of illusion it could never know anything. And so, turn away from what you perceive and reawaken, Son of God!

The miracle is merely an instant when the world is overlooked and for that holy moment a touch of heaven dawns on you and your sister and brother together. They are as natural as you would be without your misperceptive dreaming. Literally, every time you think you are participating in either a happy dream or a nightmare.

But as long as you are dreaming you have not fully awakened. Only the happy dream leads to awakening because it recognizes the dream while within the dream. This is the first step from hell towards the light of Heaven. You will fail this step many times at first. But do not be discouraged because God already promises your success.

You cannot fail to remember any more than God will at some point succeed in reminding you. He has never really stopped reminding you. You have merely chosen not to listen. You have been too busy making a home in hell to be bothered with true joy. Yet joy has not left you because it is a very real part of your own creation. Your life is joy, even though you often reflect life as drudgery, but only because you are so used to trying to make the best of darkness. And this is the nightmare you so much want to awaken from. Why, little child, will you not simply take my hand of forgiveness and awaken again into Heaven?

Change your mind about the world and what you decide in each of your decisions. The miraculous decision always forgives first. The rewards of forgiveness are always some form of true happiness. You cannot lose with such a decision. And I will always help you decide when you are not sure. Ask me, and through me the Holy Spirit will enliven and enlighten you, over and over again until God takes the last step Himself.

The world of God is Heaven. And the best news: Heaven is already in you. You need do nothing to find your holy Home except forgive what can never be your home. God will give to you your revelation, as you are prepared through each miracle to receive His full enlightenment.

And you will not believe what you have been missing, but only because it requires no belief to fully experience it. Heaven is real, as are you. God does not need to believe in you since He created you. You are His as He is yours.

Remember this and know this always, for in this realization you are indeed free. Be still, little child, and know that I AM God. And for forever, you are with me.

ON
OTHER LIFE
AND
WORLDS

It must take great effort and some pain to believe that only life on the tiny planet earth could exist!

There are many places you are not even aware that you have been. And many more that at some point you will, without a doubt go to. Did you think you arrived where you are at now by accident? Everything and everyone has a plan because everything and everyone is part of God's Plan.

You will evolve emotionally just as you will change physically, but a part of you will always stay the same. This is your creation. This is the You that has always been and will always be. You are very small yet incredibly large. You are indeed capable of flight even though you have limited yourself for the most part to the ground.

You cannot really imagine how great you are because your mind can never grasp the infinite. You do not know how much love you have within you because you learned in time to sell yourself short. And if you were to fully remember, you would not remain a slave to the world for very long.

Yet you cannot escape your own slavery by destroying your body or hiding from it in some way. You must acknowledge your seemingly endless bondage to first loosen its strings. Then, little by little, you must chip away at the bondage by learning how to constantly and consistently forgive.

If you resist the mission God has given you, the intensity will only increase and you will find yourself in a quagmire. Though uncomfortable, this will eventually teach you to forgive as well. Your choice is therefore limited as much as it seems you are free to decide. You must eventually forgive.

At some point every world seems to end. That is because at some point it seemed to just begin. Few question the validity of such a world until it gets them into some form of trouble. Then they often begin searching for another greater world, a place without limits and hatred and fear. This is as natural as you are. If it doesn't happen, something has gone wrong! It is as natural to seek the truth, as it is to love. In fact, they are indeed the same!

Some say the world ends the moment someone truly loves another. This is so true indeed! The trick is making the moment last forever. This you cannot do, and so, God has done it for you. Can you ever live in an ideal world such as this? You already do. For if Heaven is real, the world has never really occurred. Such is the perfect solution of a perfect Creator.

Are there other worlds that don't really exist? The ability to dream, little child, is as unlimited as you are! God has given you everything and nothing to make and do as you will. Yet you are limited in your ability to make your illusions more important than love.

Suffering is not a part of Heaven, but it is a part of your dependency on that which is unreal. And suffering is what you do when you fail to love. You cannot pretend that you are not dependent on the loveless. What you cannot love is all around you through your own inventiveness. It can distract you from pain and suffering, but it cannot heal it. It can seem to fulfill you, only to widen the deepened hole later. You cannot but admit that your one real need is to heal. And to heal is to heal with everyone or not at all.

It is a nice idea to think of the possibility of other worlds and places where living is easier. But it will never get any easier until together you each address the real problem and receive the real Answer together. It is so selfish to believe that you can't achieve this! You have had world wars—wars that oppose every inch of your being. And in which everyone gathered together to fight against another, seriously threatening your freedom.

Why is it that you always do your best when things are at their worst, instead of doing your best when things aren't all that bad? It is very easy to fall asleep on guard duty on a quiet night. Yet look what can happen while you are sleeping!

It is nice to fantasize about other worlds that may be better or worse than your own. Yet you are not asked to heal any world but the world you made and believe in. God has not given you the task of healing the whole universe. Merely allow healing to gently cover what you have made that is not lovable. That is the only world in need of healing. That is all you need acknowledge and do. Every world that needs healing is but a dream without love.

ON
GLOBAL
WARMING

Will you accept your part in the healing of the world?

Forging ahead to the finish line with special interests, and finished will we be. Or, the recognition that unity brings healing. Unity is only recognized and experienced as we are willing to relinquish the thought of separation back to within the Thought of Oneness.

Global warming is the lack of recognition that you are indeed a healer in your oneness with the Healer Within. A healer forgives, a healer transforms darkness into light and a healer recognizes love and spreads it into the whole world releasing it from every form of hatred. The Healer Within cannot be both a destroyer and a creator with God.

The Real Healer Within only heals, and, only the world is in need of healing, for in its true healing is its true death, and thusly, the journey back into Eternal Life in Heaven. The ego belief that "I am separate from God," false belief that it is, is the reason the ego cannot perform healing.

False gods are merely illusions that are, through fear, ego motivated, but attempt to present themselves as the God for Who one seeks. Their attempts to heal the world are misguided and prevent healing, often in the name of healing, mercy and forgiveness.

You are a healer. The ego destroys, punishes, circumvents, presupposes and hates its own fear. You are a healer. The current state of the rivers, streams, glaciers, water, earth and sky of the world are a reflection of the fear of God held within the ego mind. These perceptions merely emphasize the ego's wish to see and keep your mind and heart separate from God.

You are a healer. The "I" of the ego cannot accept the Healer Within, so it perpetuates destruction and littleness in its own defense. The ego is so intent on winning the battle against God that it would rather destroy the body and itself in the process instead of bowing gently away and admit defeat. The world destroys itself when utilized by the mind unaware of our communion with God. Yet in light there is no defeat! God or your Self can never be defeated for They can never be attacked! We have a choice.

The purpose of the Healer Within is to bring comfort through offering the Peace of God; perpetual comfort through your practice of constant forgiveness. In forgiveness the world is healed and all of its makings, including its self-destruction. Forgiveness heals because it reveals love and love reminds us of our True Nature, of the True Nature. Global warming is the separated mind on the verge of inevitable breakdown.

Our attempt to heal the earth is a demonstration of willingness to allow Spirit Within into our minds and our hearts. As *A Course in Miracles* states, "Our tolerance for pain is high, but it is not without limit." Just as an individual comes to realize that her way is guilt ridden, vengeful and cursed by itself, in this recognition and the malaise it brings, spirit brings forth willingness to receive healing.

The question becomes: Are you willing to allow the Healer Within to bring forth healing into the world? Those who truly seek the healing of the earth are recognizing the separation from the mind of God on some level of awareness even though God may not be in the forefront of their awareness. It does not matter. Only your little willingness matters.

The ego fears retaliation from a punishing God for having run away from creation. The world was made up, like the body, as a "home" for the separated mind. Just as the ego needed a body to make itself appear as real, so it needed a physical earth upon which it could exert influence, power and control. The body and the earth justify the "reality" of the ego, for the ego needs this justification, or it may, only in its own illusory mind of course, become prey of a punishing God. The ego mind is using this earth to defend itself against its own guilt and greed that will never see enough. And such is the outcome of defense.

Holy Spirit, the Healer Within, can use every form the ego has made up to bring healing into the world if there is a willingness brought forth for healing. Sometimes the body is beautiful, glowing and radiating the light of spirit. Other times it is decaying, decrepit and lingering in the pain of separation. So it is for Mother Earth. For it is either a home for separation, literally being dismantled or a temporary temple of love literally being joined.

As we allow the Healer Within to heal our projection of darkness which takes form in thoughts of condemnation, suffering, victimization, judgment and unworthiness, global warming will subside. Mother Earth is now our way Home and we will arrive Home as our hearts and minds give the very love they are always receiving from Love Itself. With this giving and receiving of love, Mother Earth will be healed and will provide for us abundantly as we journey Home. She will now experience abundance as she gives abundantly. Just as the mind communicates loving thoughts through the body, so the mind communicates and reflects these quiet and gentle thoughts as well, through the earth. The ego will use the body and the earth to communicate hell; hell being the state of the mind seemingly separated from its Creator. The Healer Within is willing to use the body and the earth to communicate only Love.

Mother Earth is but a reflection of the mind living in a stagnant state of constant change, the ego forever reinventing itself in its attempts to stay "alive." Mother

Earth is revealing to us the battle of illusions and the quest for meaning in a meaningless world. Her sinking slowly into the illusion of destruction is the ego's fear of retaliation from God; you but attack yourself.

The fearful ego-self so fears a punishing God that it will destroy itself first to avoid Him. The earth demonstrates willingness and kindness, fear and attack, as she is simply a body; a weapon of fear or an instrument of peace; a projection of fear or an extension of our Love. Ironically, she portrays both possibilities, to war against illusions—a lost battle until the end of time, or, the beauty of our True Nature flowing in the grace of God.

As all the separated minds return Home, one by one into Oneness, the body and the earth your body walks upon will no longer be needed. There are two paths Home. We walk both. The first one is the path of ego; destruction, illness, and joyless dreams and nightmares. We walk this path until our limit for pain is reached. The second path is the path of willingness to be taken another way by the Healer Within, the Way of Love.

We can learn a lot by observing the ego. You can see how the making of the body and the earth were the ego overcompensating for its error of leaving Creation. Rather than "cut its losses," admit it made an illusory mistake, and return willingly to the Lap of God, as the prodigal son returned to his father, in its deep guilt and embarrassment it made up an entire world and body for itself.

What we learn from this is how often we would rather justify our perceptions, defend them to the end and even rally to attack, rather than just admit our misperception early in the game and turn to the Healer Within to be shown the truth. There is only one choice in every moment; to make up and perpetuate the misery or to co-create and extend love with the Healer Within. Which do you think is the only real choice, precious one?

ON
WORLD PEACE

Each and every one of you will know and experience peace together one day, even though until this transition occurs, it will seem far off, like an idealistic and impossible dream.

When the transition occurs, there will be a most joyous and gentle shock that resounds throughout Heaven. When this occurs, not only will peace prevail, but it will also be recognized that humanity is truly unlimited in its scope of holy healing and creative ability.

That will be the shock: discovering that when joined together in purpose on a planetary scale, there will suddenly be such marvelous, incredible, and even at first, unbelievable potential possibility, that you will find all this rather startling. Part of this will be because of the immeasurable gifts suddenly bestowed upon you, and the other part is because it will have seemed to take so much time to realize the treasure chest that was with you all along!

Each of you has within you the inkling that what I say is true, and the great hope to someday experience it as well. And you will. Healing is what you all are struggling to achieve. But in all the complication you've forgotten that this is the one goal of being here.

If there could be tears in Heaven, it would be this forgetfulness that made it so. The hatred, the punishment that is its result, and the whole idea that evil is somehow in competition with good, has made you all lose track of your purpose together, and thus to forget the Love that truly joins you, and that is you forever.

There are many perceived barriers that seem to be preventing expediency toward the goal of world peace.

And yet each of these limitations are illusory, and can be tracked back to one original mistake: the idea that to have, you must get instead of give. It would be far better for each of you to first own nothing of the world and recognize you still have everything, than it would be for you to seek to own what you see as "everything" and thus fail to recognize there is nothing to lose.

Your possessions are nothing, and your heart is everything. The world you see in conflict is but a picture of your own idea of scarcity I have just described. Until you all help each other to recognize together that having is giving and not getting, the conflict and upheaval will continue, just as it has for thousands of your years.

The question is, when will you all be ready to give your thinking and seeing to me instead of all the fearful and death-related perceptions you are so reliant on to keep you angry and sad? When this happens, you will see a progression toward discovering true peace. When you are all truly willing to give to all, then will you most certainly receive it for everyone. Not until. Are you getting angry or giving love today? And are those not the only two goals available to you?

And yet there is only one real goal because there is only one real Answer. As long as there seems to be two, then the conflict must seem to remain. In only the giving can the real Answer be remembered. That is why peace must be found together. In receiving the Love that is offered through your relationships, it is thus given to everyone else as well. Thus it is joyously recognized that there is nothing else to attain. You have it all. For God has given it to you already. And I do speak for your will and God's.

Remember this: peace is the natural inheritance of all God's children. When they do not know peace, they do not know themselves. Honestly then, ask yourself, "Do I really want only peace?" If you want other goals before the goal of peace, then you have placed other gods before me. I do not suffer. Heaven does not suffer. The angels do not suffer. Only you suffer because you have chosen unwisely. You can have the things of the world. But do not cherish them ever above Love, or they indeed will sting you.

True communication is but a form of true giving. It is always truly helpful to love another without expectations. You can only help yourself by offering help to another. The help you offer him is merely his reminder to extend help to another. And so on. It requires few, or no words at all. It is the action that has eternal meaning. And the re-action will be your own encounter of a true miracle. This is what you came here to accomplish.

World peace is God's one goal for His Children. And shared joy is its one result. The goal is simple but the path narrow. To truly help and give is, indeed, the only decision to really make. And you made this decision when you took birth. Remember it now.

ON
GENTLENESS

Gentleness and holiness are an extension of God through his creation.

You are created from gentleness; it is your being. From holiness comes innocence, and from innocence comes gentleness. By now you are beginning to recognize your own purity. In spite of your stubbornness to accept what you are, instead of believing in what you are not, you are starting to experience a hint of light and a touch of purity that is both childlike and ancient in you. In its grandeur you are beginning to truly heal.

An illusory part of you rejects the gift that is being offered to you, while the truly Holy Aspect within you knows without a doubt and rejoices in that what I am reflecting to you is also the shining spirit of what you indeed are. You can try to deny this by hiding behind grandiosity for a while, but you have already come too far to fully reject the grandeur that you are created from.

It is now in your best interest to receive and accept fully my message to you. Receive the gift of guiltlessness and rejoice that there is no other reality than eternal joy!

To receive your holy gentleness, merely offer only this gift to others. The guiltless are free from darkness and death because they have remembered the great and gentle heart of their Creator. His loving Will comes to any mind that has chosen to be ruled by a kind and loving heart.

The humble are the lambs of God because they are truly humbled by the presence of infinite Life everywhere and within everyone. They see not the world because healing has come to replace their faded nightmares and so they cherish the world no more. Their smiles are genuine because they know they have come back Home where truly they realize they have never left. Indeed, as messengers of light from a Holy Heaven they have left fear and guilt far behind. What need have they of either, when the journey without a distance has been discovered again! Behind them is no path, in front only gentle awakening to their return Home

The search is over. The endless has come to replace the end; the changeless come to replace all change. Without further searching all that is left is to rejoice in each new and present miracle. Here is where time ends and serene smiles return to genuflect to everyone what has finally been remembered.

Every teacher of God becomes naturally and sincerely gentle with each new and present miracle. The miracle fortifies your own commitment to all creation. A religious experience is more important by far than any religion, simply because it transcends all that has been said or ever written.

The holy experience leaves time behind and embraces each and every new instant, and sees each one as another new opportunity to awaken and allow a little light from Heaven to shine the world away again. With each new miracle the world disappears a little more.

In each new instant free of thoughts of the world, Heaven opens up a little more, gently nudging the mind to give up its misperceptions and return again to the safety of the heart that lives forever within. How small the world becomes to those who would awaken to the Heart of Heaven. And how immense becomes the call of Love once heard truly!

Gentle child, you are the eternal light shining unto the world and reawakening every heart and mind like the sun awakens the flowers and the birds! Let your heart-light shine through with all of Heaven's compassion and joy. There is nothing left to fear because the world disappears as you and your companions reawaken to eternal Life together!

The end is merely a new beginning to a Life of great grandeur forgotten for only a moment. In this forgotten moment it seems as though time rolled out like a long carpet. Yet this carpet of so many colors and seeming comforts is not lasting. It can only exhaust your misdirected and devoted mind, failing to bring you its promise of rest and serenity. It must fail not because of what it is, but because of what it could never be. It is temptation. It is delusion. It is fear of death. It is hatred disguised as love. It is indeed nothing disguised as something. And it will only leave you without hope and desolate.

Leave it behind! Turn away from temptation, and take the ancient, but soft Hand I am now offering. It will lift you. It will sooth you. It will keep you and never leave you, as it never really has. Abandon this gentle Hand no longer. His Smile is resting upon you now. Would you not receive them both as my Gift to you? I would tender His Hand into yours, never to leave you again, but to keep you in the forever safety of His Comfort and His Home.

ON

YOU,
SELF-WORTH,
LOVE AND
GOD

There is nothing about you that is unloving, little child.

You are indeed young at heart even if you seem old by the world's standards. There is no measurement for what you are. Indeed, you are as ageless and timeless as Heaven because you *are* Heaven.

There is no loneliness within you that really exists. When you seem lonely it is only because you have forgotten your birthright. You are born of Heaven and can never be forgotten by anyone.

Every angel knows you and they have always been with you; even when you wanted aloneness you rested on their quiet shoulders. They are your brothers and sisters who support you and know that they are safely Home.

You have forgotten your Home, but only because you chose perception as your reality instead of Knowledge. You did this to forget Heaven and wander alone for a while in dreams.

You still cherish the dream because you choose it over your awareness of your real Self.

You are still attracted to pain and suffering because you still insist on sifting through it over and over again, determined to somehow find your lost happiness and joy in the maze. You will soon tire of this. And this will be a turning point for you. For acceptance is the first step to renewal and away from the tired and poor.

You are so valued by your sisters and brothers in Heaven. Without exception, everyone in Heaven and seemingly on earth wait for you to awaken and remember. You are holding the missing link to the gate of Heaven. Without your hand joining with all, Heaven cannot know its completeness.

Yet Heaven is complete because you are complete and only your forgetfulness would attempt to convince you otherwise. But do not forget that God's Atonement (undoing of guilt and fear) was completed the moment it was thought that the separation took place.

I have come to fulfill God's Will for everyone by reminding you that my will and your own are indeed the same. No one really wants to be unhappy although this is often what you ask for. Not knowing what true happiness is, you often search without You. This is your first and only real mistake. Nothing can be found where nothing exists!

ON
PLAYFULNESS

Laughter and gentle playfulness are sure signs that you are allowing your mind to return to the heart of Love.

The heart of love in you always calls for you to return your awareness to the playfulness within true innocence. Your heart is the part of your mind that remains light, gentle and calm amidst all turmoil.

You know when you are in touch with this God-given Reality because it literally is Heaven. Nothing about Heaven takes even the slightest intimation of the world seriously, naturally, because Heaven does not see the world. You can and must learn this kind of overlooking observance. It is this practiced overlooking that will bring you back in touch with your one light and joyous Reality.

Heaven is light and always gentle because it is your Home and God's. There is no compromise here because no darkness or seriousness can take the place of God's angels' Home. It is your Home, too, because you are an angel, dear one! Do not accept other dark and defined perceptions of your Self or your Home. It is sure, safe and as constant as God's loving Will. Let His Will speak to what you are and what you have with Him. Then, and only then, can you know your own will and your purpose for coming to earth.

You came simply to remember, and remember you will, as you allow the lightness of each miracle to be passed through you and into all others and the world. The world will not end with terror but with Love. How else could you awaken from your nightmares? Love is your Home and your one inheritance. Playing in light is but an expression of this love and willingness to but reawaken.

The world is but the opposite of awakening. Yet unconsciousness does not really exist except for those who want nightmares instead of happy dreams. But who would want nightmares over happy dreams except for the insane? The drama of nightmares is indeed a temptation to everyone, yet they cannot suffice for the children of God's Light and Love. And tiring of them will come. And the desire for a more sufficient Solution will come. You were created for happiness and joy because you are eternal light.

Light belongs to the Universe because although it can't be seen with eyes or heard with ears, its constant and happy call has never left you. It is your created desire to return to the peace of God's eternal Will. Nothing else can come close to offering you any real serenity. Although this has not stopped you from searching in many empty corners, you will and must give up this extraneous search eventually for His One simple Solution.

Let it be now instead of later. For Christ is always gently smiling as He greets you finally on your most willing return. For He is your brother and He openly shares His Kingdom with you now. He waits only for you to accept His Gift by sharing it with others.

His promise to you is the same as your promise to everyone. You come to heal, rejoin and rejoice. Is anything really more desirable than this Gift? Accept it in lightness and allow His lightness to extend to everyone through you. It is your decision to have Him do all the rest through you.

The time for childlike innocence to return on earth is come. But you must demonstrate this expression in very real terms for yourself and with everyone.

You do not have to search in dreams for what is yours in Reality. Accept it. Accept it fully as a gentle witness to Heaven. You cannot but succeed. For all of Heaven's Creation is with you, supporting the only holy direction left to happily choose.

Play only happy games, child of light! Every angel stands by you as you step to your enlightened goal. And every woman and man will walk with you as the spirit of Life offers each the food of Heaven as you join in His generosity with each. Do this for peace. Do this in holiness. Do this now in my Name and in yours.

ON
VANISHING
OF THE
UNIVERSE

You may feel initial fright at the suggestion of a vanishing universe.

It is not easy at first to accept the fact that nothing you see exists. The world is merely made up by every one of you. If you can grasp what I am saying you will be glad and laughter will follow. How happy are those who recognize that their dreams are but dreams and nothing more!

The universe seems real indeed. You see it outside of you, but only because you have chosen to apply your own made-up definitions to it. It is without any real definition because it is not really there. God does not call the dwelling you live in "a house." It is meaningless in Heaven. And so, what does have meaning?

Meaning applies only to what God created. Yet His meaning is beyond definition because Creation is an ongoing act of love. It never changes and it never ceases. It does not exist because it can't be defined. Yet it has being because it contains all that is real.

Thus, your Reality is beyond your perception and definition. To recognize it you must first accept that you do not understand it, nor can you see it or touch it. Yet it is You. And You are profound.

You will know you are unlimited the instant you remove your beliefs in definition and limitation. You cannot assign even a name to your Self, although we shall use the word Christ as it comes closer than many other definitions.

It is Christ who heals the mind of the deluded, who sees only the world as real. His eternal Self cannot be found in pictures, for what you are can never be projected. Yet it can and must be shared.

Your awakening, your enlightenment, your recognition that you have eternal life is remembered through the sharing of a Self without bodily limits and physical barriers. The miracle surpasses all of these limits because it overlooks every barrier to peace and then fully embraces it.

Thus, meaning becomes your willingness to have love extended through you to everyone. In whatever form the miracle comes it always reminds those it touches that they are indeed one with each other, our Self and God.

Blessings eternal to you, who no matter what, will always be a part of our Self, Christ. God goes with you with all His angels. Gently come Home, my sisters, brothers and every child. Indeed, come Home where every angel and God rejoices to greet you. I am found in you whenever you reach for gentleness.

I am always with you.

Jesus

DEAR JESUS...
FROM JOEL

Dear Jesus,

I feel as though I am successful at least in my ability to hear your Voice, Jesus. Why is it so difficult for me to manifest abundance for myself?

Dearest Joel,

The answer in a few words: you do not feel worthy. You are wonderful at helping others and listening for them as I speak, yet you pass my Voice by when I speak for you. You need to meditate often on your own self-value. You see yourself as merely a tiny ego, never able to do enough to receive My Love. You isolate and refuse to communicate My Love to others when I am right here to help you remember! You cannot do it alone. You need others.

You cannot judge one person as having a value, while you judge another as not having value. Unto the poorest of souls I shed blinding light through them. But do you wait to see it with them? Or do you judge for yourself first? Is it that you do not want love, or that you do not care? You may not want it, but indeed, you most certainly need it.

You are a stubborn case, dear Joel. You hear my Voice, yet you don't believe it is I. You even think that I am merely another hidden aspect of your own tiny ego!

Through me, you have brought so much to so many. You have no right to exclude yourself, Joel! Why do you belittle yourself when you have accomplished so much? And do you realize that by belittling yourself you are also attempting to belittle me?

I will send you a paragraph like this at a time so that your ego can be set gently aside only for a moment as you may wish. Yet consider this: each moment wasted on fear enters your mind deeper into the maze of hatred you have made! I did not make it. You did! Are you so arrogant to believe you can now undo what you have made without my help? You might as well ask me to start your car without the keys. It is just as ridiculous.

Joel, you need to work on letting me help you undo this shabby image you rely on. What good is a personality if it views life with eyes of a snake? Give your personality traits up. Become transparent. Stop relying on your own thinking and ask for my Word and my blessing. That is enough for today. Read this often.

Jesus

Dear Jesus,

Why do I have so much trouble meeting my needs financially and materially? And, what should I do to bring about abundance?

Dearest Joel,

I say "dearest" with emphasis, because you forget how dear and valuable you are to all Creation and to your own Father! Your addictions to things in the world only perpetuate this mad and dark dream. You can use things in the world without attachment by remembering that your survival is guaranteed by God. You will not die lonely or without a Kingdom, for you are saved because of what you are created from!

Do not fear death, and by this, do not fear the ways of the world, for they are but temporary and illusory in nature if you will, and you need not keep your focus there to manifest abundance and joy. In fact, you should not keep your focus on survival and things. Keep your focus on the love of God, His and your Heavenly Home, and offer this recognition to all to keep it in awareness!

You have much to do yet and to give in the place you now see as "home." Others need you to remind them of what I am telling you: that a greater, lasting Home awaits. It only awaits your firm recognition! Your awareness is what I am interested in, because what you keep as your treasure is what you offer to me and to all others. Yet I do not need the world of things and even ideas about it. Nor do you. Therefore, you must realign your heart and your mind with the Safety of Heaven, a Place beyond material wealth, yet so much wealthier!

If you ask me, even if it is every five minutes, I will patiently remind you of that Safety you so seek and truly need. With this firm commitment to a firm Cause, you will indeed reawaken to what you are and What you have. I can promise this, because only this is real. Will you accept my Compassion as your own? It is our perfect Spirit that you want and need. And only this will fulfill you.

If you place God's Kingdom first in all things and in your single awareness, a miracle happens: everything falls into place and you experience joy again! The joy will go out to others, and they will come to you to help you as you are willing to help them! Do you understand this? You are not dependent on the world; you are dependent only on the God you share. Take rest in this recognition and hold it in mind and heart.

I have much more for you, as you are willing to listen. I take your life and its outcome very personally, Joel, for you are doing something few can do: you are listening to me for the world! Is this not a worthy cause? And should you feel anything but worthy to receive this? I think not, and you do this very well! That is why I am with you. I can help save you grief, and I am by your side in all things. Listen more, Joel, for your own salvation. This is what you must do, then you can share it with all. Of course, I will always help you my dear brother!

Jesus

Dear Jesus,

I have been locked in this money struggle now
for many years, always barely able to make ends meet.
I know I am worthy of abundance, at least consciously.
Is there something I am overlooking?

Dearest Joel,

Of course there is something you are overlooking! Your Self worth! It is not based on what I tell you, or even what others tell you. But you often take outside input too much to heart. You look at where you live and see desolation and despair. Have I not told you that appearances deceive!

Everywhere there is richness, but you must look into your own soul and then out into the souls of others. You share this richness with them. Light is abundance! And where light is uncovered, richness abounds!

It is up to you, Joel, in so far as how you perceive. But do not look to your own picture of the world, for it must fail you because this picture has no light, no God, no Love. Remember I have said that perception is temporary. Therefore, it is illusory. You want love and knowledge, and to obtain this reality, you must give the knowledge of love. This requires that you put your own healing first in line. Do what you must do to reach beyond your own heart and into mine. This may not sound easy, but remember, I am by your side at every moment!

Listen within and do not see the world as your home. It is not, and it will always tear your Self worth down if you look at it as anything but illusion. I am not illusion, nor are you. Look within to the love and joy that you are in eternity. There and only there can you be happy.

You must practice this often, and it eventually will become second nature.

Ask for my help more often. Make it a habit stronger than eating. Then you will find real food, real love, and me with the Father loving you and holding you in perfect Safety! Do this, Joel, and life will change! I promise you this, for I have never failed you or the world and all your sisters and brothers!

LOVE Jesus!

Dear Jesus,

*As I meditate more, I realize that my mind is
preoccupied with past fear thoughts about being
homeless and without support.
Can you tell me simply how I can remember
the truth of abundance and your support?*

Dearest Joel,

You are not a body, for if you were you would indeed BE homeless! Your focus on survival seems to be important because you believe that without thinking about what steps you need to take next to avoid being "homeless" and "hungry" you will find a way to overcome being and feeling "poor."

The problem is simply that you focus on what you see as a "problem," and you therefore DO NOT focus on the Answer! Stop focusing on the problem, for it is merely the ego's attempt to keep you locked into past and future misperception! None of your perceptions are even close to being valid! Validity is discovered the instant you give all past and future perceptions to me so that I can replace them with the simple truth.

You are completely free and do not realize it. This realization comes to a mind and heart, which has fully resolved to give up the judgment, and thus the "fear" that you feel. You feel it is real. You are frightened because you are holding on to shreds of past and future pain and fear. These perceptions are fully without value and validity. You are not really living when in this state of mind.

This is the great problem of the world. You cannot act on a perception that is based entirely on fear, because if you do you merely roll up the back of the dark carpet, and then place it right back in front of you. You have no right, and no authority, to make such a judgment. And then acting on it is merely a second mistake that can only hurt your ability to heal and be free. It is self-centered, self-defeating and entirely useless to you, because it is a broken tool that can never be repaired. Throw this tool away and do not reach for it again in the trash you have placed it in. It is trash. Let it be. I cannot help you if you insist in deciding for yourself what you think is in your own best interest. You do not have an inkling of what IS in your own best interest!

The support you need cannot be seen or touched. It is spiritual and non-material. Yet it will meet and exceed all materialism, because it does not acknowledge the material world. Love cannot heal the world and its seeming lacks. Why? Because the world has no reality in truth. What healing is needed is the healing of your mind only.

Nothing outside you exists because God did not create it! GET THIS! God has no authority over illusion. The material world IS ILLUSION! Why would your Father acknowledge something that is not created or creative!? He wouldn't, because it is not essential, unimportant, and entirely useless! Your Home is good, joyous, complete in its safety of you, and unlimited in the power to over-come all things! Do not address what you think you "see" as "the problem." Address the simple fact that you have chosen wrongly in perception, and THEN, ask me for divine interference and thus, HELP!

You have no ability whatsoever to evaluate appro-priately. If you had even an inkling of divine ability, indeed, you would surely laugh out loud at the entire absurdity of your perceived dilemma! I offer you this joyous distinction, and you must simply be willing to share it.

You were asked by a homeless person today for money for bus fare. You had money, yet you only gave her a dollar when you could have covered her cost by simply asking someone for change. You made this decision and later realized it was a fearful one. Had you asked me what to do, I would have told you to give her the five-dollar bill you did not have change for. I am not concerned with your selfishness. The selfishness is merely an indicator of your lapse in total consciousness.

For a moment, you decided what was best for both of you. Then, a few moments later, you realized that you could have helped her by giving her more than she asked for. What would this have done for you and her? You would have awakened together, into an instant of total forgiveness and non-judgment! These small intervals out of time are what you need and really, you only want.

Why did you deny this for both of you? Because you thought for yourself, and then, you made a wrong decision—FOR YOURSELF! How can I help you if you won't adhere to the material I am sharing with you, Joel WRIGHT! ? WRONG!! I am not scolding you. I just want you to stop thinking for yourself and reawaken to your true function!

You know that sharing is a part of your function, because in sharing you are automatically forgiving and blessing. Often you DO do this now. Much better this year than last. I commend that you are indeed growing in your ability to listen more carefully. Yet I will that you know, YOU CAN DO EVEN BETTER. And you must do better because you represent my voice—not just in yourself, but in all others as well. Do you understand, Joel? I am the Christ! And as Christ, I am in you all as your one Self. You can only be aware of this through giving and forgiving without condition or judgment!

Tomorrow your assignment is to give to three others without judgment or condition. It is simple. But I want you to be aware of what happens to BOTH of you when you act in this way. Look in this other person's eyes, and in that instant, see the Christ that you are together.

I am not here to read or send you merely words and sermon. I am here for you to act on Christ's behalf, so that you can know of your Self and God. You can know Heaven. But you must act out of Heaven's abundance and stillness if you are to live and experience God's expression of true joy. This is your assignment! It is not difficult, except to the little ego! DO IT!

We will speak of your experience tomorrow night. I leave you in peace, in Heavenly abundance, and gentle, silent unspeakable joy. That is what I share with you in this message tonight. Do not deny my Gift. Share it. We will again talk soon, Joel Wright.

ON

PRACTICING
THE CYCLE OF
HEALING

"A Little Willingness is Truly Helpful"

Dear Holy Spirit and Jesus in Christ,

You have given Joel, others and myself answers to life's questions, insight on the ways of the ego mind and the world and visions beyond the body and this world. What are we to do with all of this? We are taught in *A Course in Miracles* to teach others what we have learned that we may truly learn it, and to give, as it is in our giving that You and our joy are increased.

I read these words of truth, love and wisdom and of the visions You have shared and appreciate their value. Joy rises in my heart when I hear truth, absorbing it into my very being fulfills like nothing else and perhaps even a spark of inspiration erupts. Then I return to my habitual thinking and ways of living, rather than allowing the effect of truth—Love—to manifest in my life. I hear and see the immense healing power of Love again and again, yet continue to return to the amnesia of the mind clinging to separation.

The search for Love continues. I tell myself I want real change and happiness in life and the world, yet turn away the very moment it is offered, which is every moment, indeed. I come into awareness of profound peace within and then later catch myself wishing it served some concrete purpose in the world like volunteering at the local hospital. I forget all who are being healed in that moment of peace, all minds being served, as all minds are joined. Why the resistance to accepting truth as reality and lack of vigilance in willingness to choose the oneness of Love over the separation of fear?

Whether we have experiences of seeing the Reality behind the veil of this world ourselves or hear of those who do, we often treat these experiences as if they are irrelevant to our everyday lives. We experience the practicality of sharing love in our comings and goings and we learn from others' experiences the real change brought forth by extending love, yet most of the time we do not put it into practice. I make excuses, "Oh, I forgot to ask Holy Spirit how to see this, how to be truly helpful." What is an excuse, but a made-up reason in defense of the ego? I do what I decide to do! The reason I "forget" is because I am unwilling to remember and I am not determined enough in my desire to experience freedom.

> Under the ego's dark foundation is the memory of God, and it is of this you are really afraid. For this memory would instantly restore you to your proper place, and it is this place that you have sought to leave.
> *ACIM, Ch. 13, III, The Fear of Redemption*

I can be resistant to willingness and weak in my determination. *A Course in Miracles* is clear that Holy Spirit asks only for our willingness and determination.

> The holy instant is the result of your determination to be holy. It is the answer. The desire and the willingness to let it come precede its coming. You prepare your mind for it only to the extent of recognizing that you want it above all else. It is not necessary that you do more; indeed, it is necessary that you realize that you cannot do more. Do not attempt to give the Holy Spirit what He does not ask, or you will add the ego to Him and confuse the two. He asks but little. It is He Who adds the greatness and the might.

He joins with you to make the holy instant far greater than you can understand. It is your realization that you need do so little that enables Him to give so much.

ACIM, Ch. 18, IV, The Little Willingness

Instead of willingness, I blame the ego for compartmentalizing holy instants in a world all their own, appearing powerless over the "real world" I wake up to every morning.

Hence, because the ego has filed them away, I forget their transforming power and I forget to be willing for more holy instants. Compartmentalizing these experiences of the reality of God, compartmentalizing everything, is exactly what the ego thought of separation prescribes, but it is my choice to take the prescription.

I blame the world for discouraging holy instants by evaluating them as "mystical" experiences only available to a chosen few, both revered and held in suspicion and they do not avail themselves to scientific observation, hence are considered invalid until proven valid. Blaming the ego and blaming the world, this is funny, like "The devil made me do it!"

Who does blaming anyway, ego or Holy Spirit? What is the ego but that part of my mind that willingly decided to run away from Home and continues to do so. What is the ego, but the thought of separation from God that has no power to rule my willingness, desire and determination, unless I allow it! The ego thought system has its own desires and determinations, but I am not the ego. I am spirit. Spirit am I. I can choose the ego to block my awareness of the absolute practicality of truth, believing that if I was to realize and accept that I am in the world, but not of the world, this will reap tremendous havoc on my world. Or I can be willing to let Holy Spirit be my Teacher and experience tremendous healing of my world.

> Selfishness is of the ego, but Self-fullness is of spirit because that is how God created it. The Holy Spirit is in the part of the mind that lies between the ego and the spirit, mediating between them always in favor of spirit. To the ego this is partiality, and it responds as if it were being sided against. To spirit this is truth, because it knows its fullness and cannot conceive of any part from which it is excluded.
> *ACIM, Ch. 7, IX, The Extension of the Kingdom*

I am beginning to stop believing in the ego's organizational structure; hierarchical, divisive and using the past as its frame of reference to guarantee a future just like it. I am beginning to trust my willingness and Holy Spirit instead.

> Trust not your good intentions. They are not enough. But trust implicitly your willingness, whatever else may enter. Concentrate only on this, and be not disturbed that shadows surround it. That is why you came. If you could come without them you would not need a holy instant. Come to it not in arrogance, assuming that you must achieve the state its coming brings with it. The miracle of the holy instant lies in your willingness to let it be what it is. And in your willingness for this lies also your acceptance of yourself as you were meant to be.
> *ACIM, Ch.18, IV, The Little Willingness*

The Voice and Eyes of Love are real and their purpose is to return our awareness to the reality of Oneness.

Holy Spirit, Christ, help us to accept the truth of our true nature as love, so we may be willing to choose love over fear and experience a change into Reality in everyday life. Now, tell us how.

I speak to this world through everyone. All the time and throughout every space, I am speaking. My Heart goes with you. The Mind of God is all there Is. These words that appear on paper are not anecdotal. They do not apply to a chosen few. They apply to the world. Yet until the world admits the terrible bind it has gotten itself into, I cannot be heard, understood, or put to good use.

Yet for those who are willing to admit the mess they are in or at least heading in, I will be heard, understood and used for a clear purpose in the world. As I have said, "Better to have a 'bad' day and eventually come into the presence of God than to have a 'good' day all on your own." I say to everyone, "Today is the best time to begin a healing program for yourself; do not delay."

"What is the point?" you ask. The purpose of the ego is to make Me appear useless. Therefore, I will not be seen as useful by the world. I will be tossed aside with yesterday's news.

My will for you, along with God's, is for that part of your mind that is still aware of God be used by you more frequently and the part of your mind that you "took away" from God, gradually decrease in its use. You do not have to listen to that part of the mind that thinks it left God. Here is the #1 way to use the Guidance given practically and purposefully:

#1
BE WILLING TO THINK
WITH THE MIND OF GOD

You received this Guidance through the part of your mind that thinks with God, therefore to put this love to work in your everyday life, only consider its meaning and purpose in your life with that same part of your mind. Do not look at it, analyze it and attempt to understand its meaning and purpose with the part of the mind that "left God."

This is the number one tool of the ego, the part of the mind that left God—to make its own use of the Voice for God within for its own purposes. This is an attempt to bring truth into the illusion. You must vow to not do this! Stay in the Mind of God. Ask Me to do this for you.

Step #1 will clear up a lot of confusion because it is the cause of confusion in those listening to the Voice of Holy Spirit and still wondering what to do now and why they are still confused, doubting and stuck. Rather than allowing truth to replace the illusion, they seek to integrate truth and illusion.

Step #1 does not happen without Step #2:

#2
ASK HOLY SPIRIT TO DO THIS FOR YOU

Do not expect the ego mind to give you permission to leave its compound and go play in the Mind of God awhile. The ego will never say to you, "Oh, yeah, go ahead and check out the truth, just be back by dinner!" Once you have had a glimpse of truth, the ego will offer you plenty of nothing to add to this new found truth, so that this truth no longer resembles It Self.

The ego is more than happy to lend you its two ears in two ways:
1) As a substitute for the Voice of Love; and
2) As an interpreter of the Voice for Love.

Get out of the way! Let Me lead you into the Mind of God, speak for God and explain His message to you.

Step #3: Holy Spirit will do all the work with your willingness, but it is still up to you to choose. Ask yourself this question:

#3
WHAT DO YOU REALLY WANT?

As Jesus said, "We cannot serve two masters." There are two paths and you are constantly choosing between the two every moment. Ask yourself this question and keep asking it. What do you really want? Notice who is answering the question. The ego list of wants is endless because not one of its desires fulfilled will bring you the happiness which you seek. The desires of the world fulfilled lead to nothing but emptiness in the end.

Step #4: Even if you still have a list of worldly desires you would like fulfilled, now do this:

#4
BE WILLING TO RECOGNIZE THAT GOD'S LOVE IS THE LOVE YOU WANT
My Love cannot be seen as practical and purposeful, until you recognize that you want it Above all else.

Nothing is put to good use or serves any useful purpose until we realize we need it. Until you are willing to see that the love of the world which you seek and either do not find or you find and are disappointed in, is not what you truly want, my Voice will not be recognized much less recognized as useful.

If you cannot seem to come into the place of recognizing that it is the real Love of God that you want, if there is still a block to that awareness, I will help you, if you want me to.

1. Be assured that this is what you truly want because this Love is your very Being. You want to return to your Self in God. Your ego does not.

2. Unconscious or conscious guilt and unworthiness are why you do not recognize that it is God's love you truly want and truly are.

3. You cannot forgive yourself for this unconscious or conscious guilt and resulting unworthiness. Forgiveness requires Intervention from Me, otherwise it is the ego version of forgiveness, a blind mind game that simply rearranges and replaces thoughts, but never forgives.

4. Even if you have no idea Who I AM or what the Love of God Is, be willing to give your thoughts of guilt and unworthiness over to Love for healing. Give Me the thought of separation from the One with Whom you are one. I will give the darkness

to the Light that heals. This is only illusion in which you have believed and feared; I know that, you do not. That is why I can heal it, you cannot. Love heals. The world's version of love gives the guilt and unworthiness another coat of wax. This shine wears off; the Shine of Love is eternal.

5. If you are unwilling, give me your unwillingness.

6. If you are still unwilling, try again. I am open 24/7 and you have unlimited visits.

7. In your willingness I will heal everything.

8. Now, you are forgiven for everything you think you did or you think someone else did to you.

   "All your past except its beauty is gone, and nothing is left but a blessing."
   ACIM, Ch.5, IV, Teaching and Healing

The more you experience forgiveness, the more willing you are to see that it is God's love you want, that you are.

9. Now, you are ready to practice forgiveness with Holy Spirit.

Step #5: Upon recognizing it is God's Love that you truly want:

#5

**ALLOW ME TO LOVE YOU,
RECEIVE GOD'S LOVE**

Now, rest and simply receive the Love being offered you. Be assured that God's Love pours freely into your willingness to receive It.

Step #6: With Holy Spirit, recognize that you are love by being grateful for the Love received:

#6

EXPRESS YOUR GRATITUDE

I do not need gratitude, but you need to develop your weakened ability to be grateful, or you cannot appreciate God. He does not need your appreciation, but you do. You cannot love what you do not appreciate, for fear makes appreciation impossible. When you are afraid of what you are you do not appreciate it, and will therefore reject it. As a result, you will teach rejection.

ACIM, Ch 6, I, The Message of the Crucifixion

In giving thanks for this gift of God received through Holy Spirit, you get that this is Real Love. As you express your gratitude to God, Holy Spirit, and Jesus in Christ or to Whoever you pray, in return this Love says, "Thank You," to you. In this you see that you are not alone. God is within You and You are within God. This is an experience of the Love that the ego cannot offer because it cannot receive It. It is this Love that is the only Love that can be truly given and truly received, because it is the only Love you want, because it is the only Love You Are, because It is the only Love there Is.

Step #7: Once real Love is experienced with your true Self, if you want to experience its practical, useful purpose in your life:

#7
LET HOLY SPIRIT GIVE THIS LOVE AWAY THROUGH YOU

Let Me put God's Love to work for you in your life by giving it to others. You will see the practical purpose of giving this love, once it is given. Until then, it feels incomplete. Until then, its purpose remains a mystery. Love is complete when shared. Love serves Its purpose when extended.

Step #8: I know you are still wondering how this Love being extended has a practical application in your everyday life. You will discover that when you:

#8
EXPERIENCE THE EFFECT OF YOUR SEEING WITH HOLY SPIRIT

In extending love, one sees Love. Your very nature is different. You are not the same person as before. Everyone else is not the same person as before. Everything looks different. What you deemed as important now does not seem so important. What seemed to upset you does not upset you now. What pretended to be love before, now no longer suffices. What you saw as hatred and evil is now seen in the Light of purification. Your eyes once soiled by the evil perception of separation from everyone's true Nature in God, are healed by Christ's vision seeing beyond appearances.

"Will people change?" I hear you asking. People cannot change of their own accord. The ego can

rearrange its parts, but not one rearrangement makes it whole. Holy Spirit changes people. If someone wants to remain in misperception, such is their choice. For you to misperceive them is your choice. Will people change? Do you remember a time when someone saw you truly? I remember. Many times you have been the receiver of being seen. It changed you because it reminded you of God. In reminding you of God, you are reminded of your creation. In awareness of creation, you are inspired to create.

This is the real change you seek. This change takes everyone out of the closed ego thought system and into the Changeless Heart of God. This is not the change to which you ask about in the question above. Your question was hoping for changes in the ego to make a person nice. This is not real change. The ego does "nice." It also switches over quite abruptly to hate. Only the reality of Love is the Cause of the Effect of Love. Real change is Caused when you are inspired to create. You are inspired to create when you have been seen. You can only be seen by the Eternal Love of God.

If you are willing to let Me see another for you, be assured that someday, that individual now having been seen, will look upon another in the manner of love that we looked upon them. In that moment of truly seeing, the one whom is seen truly is purified. It is in being truly seen and seeing truly that impurities rise up in purification. One is willing to receive the Love given by Holy Spirit, Christ's Comforter and is now truly seen; this same one gives love in truly seeing another and now Love is fully received by the one who gave it. This completes the cycle of giving and receiving. This is the cycle that heals.

It is inevitable that this will bring real change into one's everyday life. You do not control the whole cycle, yet your willingness to allow the vision of Christ is yours. For the one you saw truly with Holy Spirit to experience the change that Reality brings into the illusionary days of his world, this one must be willing to give the love he received in having been seen. Again, this love is given in one's willingness to let Holy Spirit direct their seeing. These are the visions of illumination that heal the world because they heal the separation in your mind. And so the cycle of healing continues as one who has been truly seen, is willing to see truly, and now another having been truly seen, is willing to see truly. Everyone carrying Love's healing into the world, one by one. Light replaces darkness.

Clearly, you see, healing is one mind at a time, always in relationship to another mind. Hence, no one is healed alone. Ultimately, no one is healed alone because there is no alone. Yet, in the world, everyone is very much alone, until the cycle of receiving > giving > receiving is begun with one willing mind. It is inevitable that the split mind will be healed, as it is inevitable that the Natural Effect of Love extended is creation. Creation therefore creates love. Forgiveness reflects love. Thus, forgiveness heals by remembering our creation as love.

This is what I meant when I spoke to you of letting your SELF be seen. (The Mentor Within, Let your SELF be seen). The ego fears these words because it misinterprets them. It misunderstands what is meant by SELF. You see this as an order to go out into the world by your self, without ME, and somehow still be able to see Love. Being that this is an impossible task, the earth literally shakes at your attempt to represent Love with hate. Fear uses your mind and your eyes and all you see is fear. Your sense of unworthiness erupts. This is not what I have asked of you. In being willing to receive My Love—being willing to let Me see you, you have now been seen truly. Now, you let your SELF be seen by seeing truly. Allowing true sight through Me. Now, impurities arise to the surface and are purified. In purification the mind is illuminated. The Light of Illumination embraces the darkness you have willingly given to It and returns it to truth. The eyes of fear are replaced with the Vision of Love. The prodigal son returns Home.

Step #9: The "Cycle of Healing" in motion, now what?

#9
EVERY SIGHT TRULY SEEN, EVERY SOUND
TRULY HEARD, EVERY WORD TRULY WRITTEN,
EVERY VOICE SPEAKING TRULY.
HOW DOES ONE PRACTICALLY APPLY THIS
LOVE GIVEN IN OUR WILLINGNESS
TO RECEIVE IT AND RECEIVED IN
OUR WILLINGNESS TO GIVE IT?
IN BEING IT, THE DOING COMES NATURALLY.
EXPERIENCE IT FOR YOUR SELF!

Excerpt from Visions of Illumination, Seeing With The Mentor Within
© 2008 The Mentor Within®

I AM BEGINNING

HOLY SPIRIT

CLOSE MY EYES

SO I MAY NOT BE SO BLIND AS TO JUDGE

WHAT I THINK I SEE

PLACE MY HANDS OVER MY EARS

SO I MAY NOT BE SO DEAF AS TO JUDGE

WHAT I THINK I HEAR

STEADY MY MOUTH

SO I MAY NOT BE SO LEARNED AS TO SAY

WHAT I THINK I KNOW

HOLD MY HAND

SO I MAY NOT BE SO QUICK TO MOVE

ON MY OWN

REPLACE MY SIGHT

WITH YOUR VISION

THAT I MAY SEE TRULY

OPEN MY HEARING

TO YOUR VOICE

THAT I MAY HEAR TRULY

SPEAK THROUGH ME

WITH YOUR WORDS

THAT I MAY TRULY SPEAK

MOVE THROUGH ME

WITH YOUR LOVE

THAT I MAY TRULY LOVE

NOW

I BEGIN AGAIN

Excerpt from Visions of Illumination, Seeing With The Mentor Within
© 2008 *The Mentor Within*®

No one better to save the world than Self
Self who is love, One Self in God
I see that now
Doing my part still, in Self

No one better to save the world than you
Do your part, in Self
Acknowledge Spirit, the heartmind of Love
In you, in everyone, indeed

Be still
Demonstrate
Believe nothing
Accept Love

Fret not over the world
Be not for it or against it
Ask for truth and so shall you receive

The power of the words within
Do not seek to mask the frailty of the world
Nor to overcome it
Neither will provide

Love instead
Watch carefully the Life and death
Within your own mind
Choose wisely

Waiting for you
My dear ones
Is Everything
It is here
It is now
Come

Mary's Vision —

I am laughing for I see
Jesus and the spirit of Joel,
one in All, emanating joy
and looking upon us all
seeing only Love,
for there is only Love to see.

Giving thanks.

I am singing Love.

In Joy,

Mary
(Rev. Mary Gerard Lenihan)

also by Joel Wright...

Ordering Information:

ISBN: 978-0-9767485-4-0
Second Edition

www.amazon.com
www.projecthealingpress.com

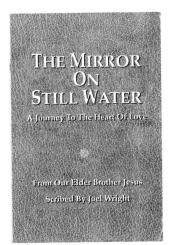

The Mirror on Still Water
A Journey to The Heart of Love

Scribed by Joel Wright

Joel scribes a collection
of Jesus' direct answers
to individuals' questions
about their personal lives
and living in the world.

Covering the range of
ego issues we face every day,
the answers are truly helpful
for everyone.

About the Author

Joel Wright listens within
for Jesus' message
and scribes what he hears,
blessing us with Jesus' voice
that is so needed
in today's world.

An excerpt from
The Mirror on Still Water

It is through your relationships that you will find God or lose God, even though in truth it is impossible to really lose Him/Her. Yet it is quite possible to forget.

The purpose of your life may seem to have many directions with many desires. I tell you it has only one; to remember the Light from which you came. You cannot remember the pure and most holy Love you came from without participating in the function God gave to you to accomplish this. Your only function is to forgive the world and all you have ascribed to it and yourself.

I do not mean by this that you leave the world and go sit in a cave and meditate. Many who have sat in darkness and looked for the light in it have not found it. Light is found only by overlooking darkness, thereby recognizing that darkness does not, in truth, exist. You can bring the Light to darkness, but you can never bring darkness to Light. You can shine away illusions with truth, but you can never bring truth to your illusions. Yet, you cannot find the light of truth and keep it without your relationships.

Each relationship is brought to you for the purpose of remembering the truth. Not one relationship has ever come to you that you have not asked for and chosen. The ones that seem fearful to you, you have asked for so that you could recognize your illusions and heal them. The ones that are loving to you are the ones you have allowed only truth and light to rest on. The latter represents your holy relationships; the ones in which you have given yourself entirely to God, and ones which will demonstrate to you beyond a shadow of a doubt how mighty the power of Love is in you both.

You will gain strength, faith and conviction in your true Self through these relationships. The former represents the doubt, the fear, the hatred, the judgment and all the illusion that you still believe in yourself to be "real."

It is these relationships; the ones that seem somehow despicable or frightening, that will ultimately bring you to the recognition experientially, that your fears, guilt and blame were never justified; that your misjudgments about them were never, in fact, true. That is why the yogi invites the demons to come in the cave and have tea with him. He does not fear what fear seems to tell him, because he knows it will avail him all the more clearly, the path to God.

It is this "risking" that the world has worked so hard to avoid. You have been taught to avoid risks and hide in the cave. Yet in this act, the outcome can only be a depressing one, for the choice to not participate with the "enemy" is the choice to place your Self out of your own heart. Your enemies are by far your best teachers, for the "enemy" is truly only your own belief that you are somehow separate from God.

That is why ultimately you must learn that there are no special or "better" relationships. Not one brother or sister who walks in this world is any less or more a teacher to you than if God Himself were to come down and walk side by side with you. All relationships have the potential to be holy ones, and until they become as such, they remain as special love or hate relationships; that is, a relationship that is either idolistic or conditional. When you are willing to take the risk with whatever areas in your life make you fearful about a relationship, you will find the gift of healing that far surpasses even your wildest of dreams!

Intimacy, my dear brother, is only your willingness to take that risk, jump off the cliff of fear, and discover the joy of God together! It is nothing more or less than what I have just described. Yet the ego will tell you that intimacy will reveal only your secrets to another who will eventually use them against you. And the ego is right on behalf of the other egos it represents. For the ego fully believes that your illusions about yourself are "real."

Indeed, you believe that if you reveal your secrets you would be demonstrating a horrible weakness that once known would consume you. And it would if you were the ego's child! But you are not, and anything the ego holds in secret will but disappear in the twinkling of an eye once it has been willingly witnessed to and brought to Light! Your relationships are there for you only to reveal the eternal to you. That is your purpose: to know and experience joy! But you cannot do this until you are willing to bring what is not joy to the light. This involves pain, but only to the degree that you resist the risk. Once an illusion is brought truly to the light by two people joined in one purpose and one function, only holiness and happiness can pervade!

Not all your intimate relationships will be successful in your eyes. To the degree you feel let down when a lover leaves you, to that degree have you not come to terms with Where your only true dependency lies. Each of you seem to leave relationships at times, leaving the other to feel abandoned with their secrets exposed and their hearts broken. I tell you, this happens only because one of you has forgotten Where all happiness lies! The one who leaves another, leaves because the other has forgotten and chosen to make illusions reality and Reality an illusion! The body and the world have become more important than God. That is why in relationship it is essential to know Where your conviction lies. If you lose sight of It, of course, the relationship must seem to fail. And yet no relationship can ever really fail, for all that was shared through Love will live in you forever. Essentially that is all a relationship can ever be—all that you share in Love. The rest is but a dream.

I will repeat this and urge you to listen. Your purpose here is to find a joy that is not dependent on the world or the things and bodies outside you. In no way can you experience this joy as long as you place value where value does not belong. Your function in this world is healing through your willingness to take the risk and forgive what you think you see in others or yourself. It is always your Self you are forgiving, and each person who you attract to you will offer you an opportunity to do this, or to project and place blame outside you where you will make it seem impossible for either of you to heal.

The choice you have is only one of two; Love or fear. And yet the choice for fear is only a choice to wait a little longer for the final and only choice, which is Love. Indeed, it is painful not to foster intimacy. You came here to love, and to love with all your heart—just as God loves you!

Do not deny God's Gift to you, It was given you so that you could know His/Her Peace. Do not be afraid to love, for it will only weary you. Listen to what your heart is telling you. Let your heart, not your mind, take the journey to Love for you!

– scribed by Joel Wright

Excerpt from *The Mirror on Still Water*
© 1997 Joel Wright

Books by Mary Gerard...

Ordering Information:
ISBN: 978-0-9767485-0-2

Pathways of Light 1.800.323.7284
www.pathwaysoflight.org
www.thementorwithin.com
www.amazon.com
www.projecthealingpress.com
TRADE DISTRIBUTION:
New Leaf Distributing Company
1.800.326.2665

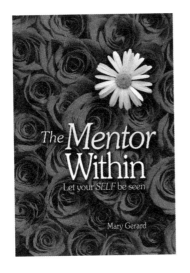

The Mentor Within
Let your SELF be Seen

by Mary Gerard

This series of conversations between the voice of ego and Voice of Self reveals the stark contrast between truth and illusion, clearly demonstrating how befuddled the ego is and how clear the Voice for God is offering release and the truth of Love that sets us free.

Mary asks a vast array of questions on relationships, life purpose, work, how to live in the world, spiritual teachers, and Jesus even drops in for a conversation to share who he is and his experience of being in the world, but not of the world. The Mentor Within doesn't mince words, gives plenty to laugh about and extends the Real Love we seek for outside of ourselves, but can only find Within.

About the Author

Mary has many worldly credentials, none of which verify her credibility as a qualified listener of the Voice of Holy Spirit. Her sincere willingness to pause, step aside, give illusions to the truth and listen to Love, moment-to-moment, are what she offers. Only our true SELF is credible because It knows who It is, because It is at one with the One Who Knows.

An excerpt from
The Mentor Within
Let your SELF be seen

Mary Gerard's questions and comments are in normal typeface
and **The Mentor Within answers in bold typeface.**

Divine Nature

There is just not enough time in the day to do all I would like. It is so disturbing. I would like more time to meditate and pray, but the world calls.

I understand your humanness and your desire to face the truth. It is all within your sense of purpose to want to benefit from divine nature, to relish your time here on earth, and to keep your eyes on God.

I know I can rest with God amidst my daily activities. But I crave silent, still, gentle time with God, a lot of time. I long for solitude.

Most of the time today that you spent with God was quite fruitful. Communion with divinity is a profound liking for you. Convincing you to focus on God even more is taking time.

What do you mean, "taking time?"

No matter what your desires and intentions, time is of the essence, and how you divide it up into its many compartments for futile activities counteracts even your good desires and so-called

intentions. Divine nature is not clocked and cannot be compartmentalized like human nature. God is not a blender. God does not take all of our desires and intentions and blend them nicely into a frozen beverage to quench our thirst. We cannot arrange our schedules and days and then ask God to intervene. God will not intervene on our plans. We may eventually self-destruct or become wealthy in the eyes of the world, and then blame or thank God, but God has nothing to do with our planned lives. God has a plan.

You no longer want to live according to the rules of this world and yet you are considering purchasing yet another appointment book to try to gain better control over your life. And it looks good, doesn't it? These nice black scheduling books so neat, organized, and personalized. If only that were your answer.

This is my prayer, "Dear God, show me how to love." It is not about being right, I want to love.

Excerpt from The Mentor Within - Let your SELF be seen
© *2003, 2006 Mary Gerard Lenihan*

Also by Mary Gerard...

Ordering Information:
ISBN: 978-0-9767485-2-6
Pathways of Light 1.800.323.7284
www.pathwaysoflight.org
www.thementorwithin.com
www.amazon.com
www.projecthealingpress.com

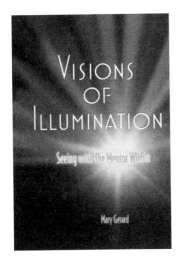

Visions of Illumination
Seeing With The Mentor Within

by Mary Gerard

A Sound is travelling through the universe at the speed of Light— a silent sound on one path through the center of all hearts and the axis of all minds. It penetrates the body of all those open to its Silence.

No matter how many years pass or come and go or are projected into the future, this Silent Light has no known beginning for it began of its Own Accord before we all knew of Beginnings. It has no end and we will each find our Life in its Light—All of us.

About the Author

Mary is willing to share her experiences of cultivating a relationship with her Inspiring Self Mind, Inspiring to Serve Love. Everything changes as we are moved from the trappings of the mind floundering in darkness to the true freedom of the mind illuminated by the Light. This relationship is the springboard to experiencing the constant direction and eternal love of our Inspiring Self in every aspect of our lives.

Our own experience of this Love is essential because then we know It is real. When we pause to Love's presence, we see Its effect on our perceptions, thoughts, choices and actions. This changes every- thing. This is the change we seek, but cannot find. It is the changelessness of Eternal Love. It is within.

An excerpt from
Visions of Illumination
Seeing with The Mentor Within

A Sound is travelling through the universe at the speed of Light—a Silent Sound on one path through the center of all hearts and the axis of all minds. It penetrates the body of all those open to its Silence. No matter how many years pass or come and go or are projected into the future, this Silent Light has no known beginning for it began of its Own Accord, before we all knew of Beginnings. It has no end. We each find our Life in its Light. All of us.

The promises of this Light bring hope into a world of despair and loneliness, to those who want it. Sooner or later everyone will want it as they realize it is all they want—Nothing would bring greater happiness to this Light. Around the corners of darkness, shadows of the past, is Illumination standing prominently in Vision. We fling ourselves into it or run around it.

A woman sees It—she runs into it for her absolute final destination, craving its security and safety so deeply. It is Eternal Love. Not how she imagined, a warm burning light to look upon and keep her warm, but a holy grail, a host to God. And she receives Eternal Love—total rest in Total Stillness. Now amidst the Light, the form of the flesh body of the illusion falls away and is replaced with light to be of true service. A light within the Light is present to welcome all those who have yet to come. Her job is essential, for in her welcoming the others fleeing into Illumination, her illumination is complete. She moves toward Home and takes her place. No one goes Home alone. We enter Illumination through the Light in one another. Illumination holds the Light for our work of forgiveness.

Though forgiveness is an illusion, it points toward Reality, Illumination, otherwise it is not forgiveness. This is possible because Reality created Holy Spirit and gave it awareness of this one illusion to help us out of the illusion and return us to Reality. The whole universe becomes meek in the presence of Illumination. Pictures of "reality" now seen as the illusion they are, fade away in their crumbled frames and torn edges and Spirit reveals Reality.

Now, I see myself, oddly enough, as an old man with flowing white hair, glowing skin, all in white, celebrating, "What a glorious day." A smile across my face and arms spread wide open. I walk in the world again on the same familiar street, anew—a new being of light. A quiet whispering so Silent I cannot help not hear, "Welcome Home, Welcome Home."

So, I didn't die after all. Here I am. Who I thought I was simply fell away in the Illumination of forgiveness.

Excerpt from Visions of Illumination, Seeing With The Mentor Within
© 2008 The Mentor Within®

How To Obtain Your Own
Personalized Scribing From Jesus:

If you would like a personalized scribing
From Jesus, through Mary Gerard,
please email your request to:

Mary@thementorwithin.com
or go to www.thementorwithin.com

Mary will choose one question each month,
being one answer answers many questions,
and post the scribing on www.thementorwithin.com

Mailing Address:
Mary Gerard
P.O. Box 9197
St. Louis, MO 63117

Thank you.

Love blesses all,
Mary